A COMMUNITY OF WITCHES

STUDIES IN COMPARATIVE RELIGION

Frederick M. Denny, Series Editor

A Community of Witches

CONTEMPORARY NEO-PAGANISM AND WITCHCRAFT IN THE UNITED STATES

Helen A. Berger

University of South Carolina Press

© 1999 University of South Carolina

Cloth edition published by the University of South Carolina Press, 1999

www.sc.edu/uscpress

Manufactured in the United States of America

21 20 19 18 17 16 15 14 13   10 9 8 7 6 5 4 3 2 1

ISBN: 978-1-61117-315-4 (paperback)

Some of the material in chapter 6 originally appeared in "Routinization of
Spontaneity," *Sociology of Religion* 1995, 56(1):49–62.

To John

CONTENTS

List of Illustrations   ix

Editor's Preface   xi

Preface   xiii

Prologue: To the Tribe Let There Be Children Born   1

Chapter 1 Background   4

Chapter 2 The Magical Self   26

Chapter 3 The Coven: Perfect Love, Perfect Trust   47

Chapter 4 A Circle within a Circle: The Neo-Pagan Community   65

Chapter 5 The Next Generation   82

Chapter 6 The Routinization of Creativity   100

Chapter 7 Conclusion   123

Notes   131

Bibliography   135

Index   143

ILLUSTRATIONS

following page 64

High priestess doing incantation during handfasting (marriage) ritual
High priestess joining together the hands of the bride and groom at a
    handfasting
High priest in ritual robes
Witch in ritual robes
Ritual altar
North altar at Circle of Light coven's 1996 Beltane ritual
Bumper sticker with the Neo-Pagan symbol of the pentagram

EDITOR'S PREFACE

Americans have come a long way from the days of the Salem witch trials in the 1600s to the present time, when practically no one blinks at the mention of fellow citizens worshiping at "alternative altars" far removed from the Christianities and Judaisms that have come to compose the mainstream of American religion. And although newer religious communities from the Middle East and Asia—for example Islamic, Hindu, Buddhist, Confucian—are also bringing doctrines, beliefs, and practices that are new to most Americans, they are nevertheless widely acknowledged to have long, respected histories in their places of origin and definitive institutional development.

Helen Berger's rich, analytically sophisticated, field-based study of contemporary Neo-Paganism and Witchcraft adds significantly to the steadily growing scholarly literature. A special dimension of her book is its placing the phenomenon in the context of globalism, wherein contemporary people can pick and choose among spiritual options in a free marketplace. During the post–World War II period in America, with some exceptions, it has been increasingly unnecessary to defer to mainstream religion or to be either furtive or brazen when following alternative meaning systems, whether that means being atheist, agnostic, or following an exotic cult.

Another notable dimension of this book is its attention to the phenomenon of routinization whereby Neo-Pagan communities are developing enduring institutional practices and traditions through experimentation and dissemination in matters such as ritual among cobelievers across the country. As founding members of covens age and have children, they are feeling the need to find ways of securing a stable future for their communities. And as these communities become intergenerational they are also having to work through morally complex, emotionally charged, and culturally as well as politically challenging issues connected with the sexual symbolism and ritual that are important dimensions of Neo-Paganism and Witchcraft.

A Community of Witches is an important milestone in the continuing development of this series. And although the data that it analyzes and interprets is fresh and intrinsically fascinating, the study as a whole may also be of considerable use for our understanding of how other new religious communities are sustaining and developing themselves in the unprecedentedly rich tapestry of American religious pluralism.

Frederick Mathewson Denny

PREFACE

This book is an exploration of the new religious movement of Neo-Paganism and Witchcraft as practiced in the United States among groups that include both women and men.[1] My purpose is twofold: to examine Witchcraft as a religion of late modernity and to analyze the aging process of this new religion. In placing the Witchcraft movement within the context of late modernity, I have been influenced by Giddens's structuration theory (1984, 1987, 1990, 1991) and Beckford's work on religions of late modernity (1984, 1992a, 1992b).

I argue that the development and spread of Witchcraft in the late twentieth century is an outgrowth of globalism. Only a modern person can stand outside of time and tradition to pick and choose elements of older and geographically disparate religious practices to combine into a new religion. Furthermore, the availability of modern technology—for example, fax machines, computer networks, and desktop publishing—has helped spread this religion.

As I will show in this book, the magical practices of Witches, while having some similarities to the practices of traditional societies, are in essence very different. Magic as practiced by present-day Witches is a "technology of the self." Although Witches do participate in magical practices to, for instance, alter the weather or effect a cure for AIDS, most of their magical acts take the form of altering the self. Similarly, I argue that the model of community that has developed among Witches differs from the traditional concept of community—that is, a geographically placed group whose members have face-to-face interactions. Instead, a global construct of community has developed based on shared interest in mysticism, magic, and goddess worship.

Witchcraft, like most new religions, has primarily attracted people in their twenties.[2] However, the earlier adherents of this religion are now in their thirties and forties and are in the process of raising children and building their careers. As I will illustrate, the birth of children to Witches is having profound effects on both the practice and organization of this religion. For instance, sex, which is viewed as a magical act, has been encouraged in interpersonal relations and at festivals. Neo-Pagans have regularly danced naked or seminaked to the beat of drums around camp-fires throughout the night at festivals. The growing number of children at festivals has brought concern about open sexuality and the need for quiet so that both the children and their parents can sleep. As I will demon-strate, the dual demands of child rearing and career advancement have led to the development of routinization.

Creating new rituals, organizing festivals, and writing newsletters are time-consuming activities. As the religion and the adherents them-selves age, there is increased interest in the development and growth of umbrella organizations. The form of routinization of this new reli-gion, while having some similarities to Weber's (1964) notion of routinization of charisma, is different. It is not the magical persona and teachings of the prophet that are being routinized by his or her disciples; instead, there is a growth of technical experts who are ca-pable of running a festival, organizing a newsletter, and editing a journal. Because individuals who are forming covens, writing rituals, or preparing magical rites are guided by Neo-Pagan journals, news-letters, and the Internet—as well as by information they have gleaned from their attendance at large festivals—there is a increased homogeniza-tion in Wiccan ritual practices and beliefs. This form of routinization is consistent with the developments of late modernity.

This book is the outcome of my participation in the Neo-Pagan com-munity since October 31, 1986; both formal and informal interviews with more than one hundred Witches and Neo-Pagans; study of the prolific body of literature written by adherents on their religious practices; and a national survey I conducted with Andras Corban Arthen, the leader of the largest Neo-Pagan group in New England.[3]

I met Andras Corban Arthen at the first open ritual I attended. I was invited to the ritual by David, whom I had met at my public lecture at the Boston Public Library, part of a series on witchcraft in New England that the library asked me to present in October 1986.[4] The lectures focused on the historical witch trials in New England, the most famous of which occurred in Salem, Massachusetts.[5] The last talk in the series, however, was about the small but growing phenomenon in present-day New En-gland of people who called themselves Witches. I had gathered my material for that presentation from the modest body of literature that then existed on contemporary American Witches (Adler 1979, 1986; Starhawk 1979; Truzzi 1972, 1974) and an interview with a woman peripherally associ-ated with Neo-Paganism.

In response to my comment that Witches looked no different than the average person in Boston, one elderly woman who had attended the entire series asked if there might be Witches in the audience. When I answered in the affirmative, she turned to the audience and asked if anyone there was a Witch. About six or seven people raised their hands. After the talk, several of those who had identified themselves as Witches came to speak to me. It was through these initial contacts that I became integrated into the New England Neo-Pagan community.

Three of the people who had attended that lecture invited me to participate as a researcher in the formation of the group they were organizing, the Circle of Light coven. For the first two years of this group's existence, I attended weekly meetings and all of the group's festivals. I have remained friendly with the founders and I continued to attend many of the coven's open rituals until it disbanded in the fall of 1996. As membership did not require that one be a Witch, I joined the organization founded by Andras Corban Arthen, EarthSpirit Community (ESC), soon after beginning my research, and I have maintained my affiliation with this organization throughout my research.[6] Membership in the organization entailed paying a fee of $30 per year, which entitled one to a monthly newsletter, invitations to open rituals and festivals, and a reduction of fees for attending those events. Through both my initial contacts and my participation in ESC events, I met a diverse group of Neo-Pagans and Witches. My contacts expanded as each new person I met introduced me to others.

I was able to interview formally more than forty Witches and Neo-Pagans. These interviews were conducted in an open-ended manner. I usually began by asking people about their family and religious backgrounds, and how they had become interested in the practice of Witchcraft. I did not adhere to a strict set of questions but instead permitted the interviewees to discuss those aspects of their spiritual or magical practices that were most important to them. My informal interviews took the form of conversations at gatherings, rituals, or festivals; I later recorded the conversations in my fieldnotes. Both the formal and informal interviews were conducted throughout the eleven-year period of my fieldwork.

The people I interviewed are from a wide variety of covens in the northeastern United States; although in some instances the interviewees were members of the same group, in most they were not. Five of the people at the time of their interviews were solo practitioners; three of these individuals had never been coven members. Because of the secrecy of groups and practitioners, I was dependent on snowball sampling, in which I either was introduced to the people I interviewed through other Neo-Pagans

I knew, or met these individuals at gatherings I attended or at public talks I gave on my research. I also put an ad in the EarthSpirit newsletter, on the Internet, and on the bulletin boards of several occult bookstores in the Boston and Philadelphia areas seeking Wiccans I could interview. I received only one response, from a man who with his wife had been trained by one of the covens I knew well. We began the interview by exchanging news about people we both knew within the Neo-Pagan community.

I was invited to participate in at least one ritual with ten different covens—all of which were in the northeastern United States. As the focus of my research has been on inclusive groups, only two of these covens were women's-only groups; the other eight included both men and women. I have attended a wide range of rituals that were organized by the Circle of Light coven and MoonTide coven, both of which are inclusive of men and women. I began attending MoonTide rituals shortly after I moved to Pennsylvania in the fall of 1991 and have subsequently continued to attend their gatherings. Throughout my research, I have attended rituals, gatherings, and festivals organized by EarthSpirit Community.

As is always the case with qualitative research, my sample was limited to a relatively small number of Neo-Pagans and covens. Furthermore, my interviews and participant observation were confined to the northeastern United States. This may mean that some regional differences within Wicca are not examined in this book. However, my qualitative research was supplemented by reading Neo-Pagan and Wiccan journals and books that have a national or even international circulation, reading on the Internet, and through the national survey I conducted with Andras Corban Arthen. Both my review of Neo-Pagan sources and the results of the survey suggest that the differences among groups and practitioners within the United States are less important than the similarities.

The survey I wrote and distributed with Andras Corban Arthen was entitled "The Pagan Census." Andras had initially hoped to do a census of the entire Neo-Pagan community. Although we were unable to achieve that goal, we did receive more than two thousand responses. The survey was distributed through Wiccan and Neo-Pagan organizations nationally, published in journals, reprinted on the Internet, and distributed at festivals. We were not able to guarantee that the survey was randomly distributed. Because of the secrecy of many Witches, neither the journals nor the Neo-Pagan or Wiccan organizations could give us their membership lists. For similar reasons, previous surveys have also not been random—they have either been local (Kirkpatrick et al. 1986) or distributed completely at festivals (Adler 1978; 1979; 1986; Orion 1995). Our survey has the advantage of including people who do not attend large gatherings. Evan Leach and Leigh Shaffer, both on the faculty of West Chester University, worked with me on the process of coding, entering data, and analyzing the materials that Andras and I collected. In addition to the quantitative questions, the survey allowed room for respondents to write freely about any questions or issues they considered important. Some individuals included several typed pages, describing their concerns for the Neo-Pagan community, their personal beliefs and practices, or a critique of our questions. These responses provide a wealth of information, although they clearly do not represent even a random sample of the population that answered our survey.

Since becoming involved with the Neo-Pagan community, I have become friends with a number of Witches and Neo-Pagans but have not myself joined the religion. I tried to make clear to every group I joined and each person I interviewed that I was a researcher, not a Witch. Because I defined myself as an outsider some people guarded what they said in my presence, although on the whole people came to accept my presence as a normal part of a gathering and were open around me. To some people that I met informally, I did not get a chance to explain that I was a researcher; these may think that I am a Witch, because they have seen me at a number of gatherings and rituals. I learned that some members of the Circle of Light coven anticipated that I would join after I learned more about their practices and rituals. An advantage of being an outsider is that I was not viewed as a member of one faction or tradition and was, therefore, often privy to both sides of disputes that developed among groups or between individuals. Furthermore, I was invited to a number of different groups' rituals.

I am indebted to those individuals within the Witchcraft community who invited me to their homes, rituals, and covens. Many spent hours speaking to me about their religious beliefs and practices. The members of the Circle of Light coven particularly, welcomed me into their circle and their lives. At the start of my research, Andras Corban Arthen invited me to attend his course on Witchcraft at the Cambridge Adult Education Center. Only through his contacts within the larger Neo-Pagan community were we able to complete our survey. I hope that in reading this book, all those who helped me will feel that they have been aptly and sensitively represented.

The Faculty Development Fund at West Chester University provided me with the initial funding to conduct "The Pagan Census." More than fifteen student workers helped code and enter data for the survey. I am also grateful to my university for permitting me to take the time from teaching to write this book. My colleagues Leigh Shaffer and Paul Stoller read early drafts of some chapters. Leigh Shaffer, along with Evan Leach, must be thanked for the hours of work each contributed to the organizing and processing of "The Pagan Census." Hugo Freund, who for several semesters had the office next to mine, was always available and interested in speaking to me about my research.

Members of my feminist study group at West Chester University—Elizabeth Larsen, Stacey Schlau, Deborah Mahlstedt, Geetha Ramanatha, Anne Dzamba, Ruth Porritt, Madelyn Gutwirth, and Jane Jeffrey—were an inspiration and a help at the early stages of this work. A number of colleagues at the Association for the Sociology of Religion and the Society for the Scientific Study of Religion have contributed their insights as I struggled through my research. Most notably Fred Denny, the editor of this series, and Madeleine Cousineau have generously given time to speak to me about my work. My research on the Covenant of the Unitarian Universalist Pagans (CUUPs) was greatly aided by my friend and former colleague Elisabeth McGregor, who is a trustee of the Unitarian Universalist Association.[7] She graciously provided me with information and contacts in the association. My greatest debt is to my husband, John H. Wolff, to whom this book is dedicated—he read every chapter and gave me unerring support and love throughout the project.

A COMMUNITY OF WITCHES

Prologue

To the Tribe Let There Be Children Born

A group of about twenty Witches has gathered at the end of August to wiccan, that is, to initiate into the faith, the newborn child of two of the leaders of the New England Witchcraft community. The group has gathered in a suburban state park, near the child's home, where it has held a number of outdoor rituals. True to Augusts in New England, the day is hot and sunny. The sunlight filters through the trees, which provide some shade and project an abstract pattern on the ground and the surrounding people. Where there is no cover the sun burns down. The child, who is a little over a month old, is kept in the shade of a tree. As the ritual is about to begin, his mother dresses him in her family's baptismal robes. The child begins to cry as his mother puts the white silk robe and pink embroidered outer-robe on him. Pictures are taken of the child with his mother, his father, and all three together. Members of the congregation joke about the child's objecting to these pictures when he turns fourteen.

As is traditional in this religion, the participants in the ritual form into a circle, in this case around a three-foot-deep hole that has been dug in preparation. Four people are asked to volunteer to call forth the four quarters (east, west, south, and north) and to explain these to the child who is entering his first "circle of power." The child's father, holding a large sword, addresses the crying child, who is held in his mother's arms near the center of the circle. The child is told that this is the first time he will walk this path, but it will not be the last. With the sword the father, while he chants a magical incantation, traces in the air a replica of the circle we have formed. The symbolic circle is formed to hold the positive energy created by the participants and to keep out all harm and evil.

The child's mother carries him around the circle clockwise, stopping first in front of the person who is calling in the powers of the east and who explains to the child that the east, whose element is air, holds the power of intellect. The spirits of the east are then called into the circle. In turn the child is introduced to the south, whose element is fire and who is the power of passion; the west, whose element is water and who is the power of emotion and intuition; and finally the north, earth, the power of life, of growth and regeneration. In turn the spirits of each of these directions, or quarters, are invited to bring their power into the circle.

After the circle has been consecrated, the father removes the child's afterbirth from a plastic bag and places it in the hole in the center of the circle. The afterbirth has been stored in the family's freezer since the child's birth. The blood from the afterbirth runs down the father's hand and into the hole. The air is permeated with the sweet smells of blood and sweat. Addressing the child, the father tells him that this umbilical cord sustained him for the nine months he was attached to his mother; now there is a new rope, a white one that will spiritually attach him to the mother of us all, mother earth. A white silken rope is dipped in the child's birth blood, which has also been kept in the family freezer awaiting this ritual. The child is anointed with his own blood, some of which splashes on his silk gowns. The remainder of his birth blood is poured into the hole, which is subsequently filled with dirt.

Throughout the ritual the participants stand, maintaining the form of the circle. They are there to witness the rite and to contribute their "energy." Each person is believed to have personal powers, whether he or she is aware of them or not, that can be used for magical or spiritual workings. Those who are cognizant of their powers have the ability to direct them and lend them to the work at hand. To further contribute their will to this wiccaning all the participants are asked to pick a piece of ribbon upon which they will make a wish for the child's future. The color of the ribbon corresponds to a particular direction and the spirits associated with it. Yellow is chosen for wishes associated with the east, or intellect; red for the south, or passion; blue for the west, or intuition; green for the north, the mother earth; and white for spirit. The child's mother requests that each person's wish be some aspect of his or her own personality that he or she wants the child to possess. For example, a green ribbon would be chosen if you wished the child a love of nature. I pick red and wish the child passion for people and for life. Most people have chosen blue, the color associated with emotions and intuition, although all the colors and hence all the elements are represented. The disproportionate representa-

tion of blue is not surprising, because within this group there is an emphasis on intuitive knowledge and inspirations. People come forward randomly
to present their wishes and tie ribbons on a branch that is held by the
mother. The last two people to tie a ribbon on the branch are the child's
parents, both of whom pick white, the color associated with the spirit.
After everyone has tied a ribbon to the branch, the circle is declared open.

A light picnic lunch is served while the participants admire the baby,
and his mother opens the gifts that people have brought for him—baby
blankets, clothing, and toys. Several people note how much the child looks
like his father, who has said that he felt his wife was giving birth to him as
he saw his son emerge from the womb. I overhear a discussion of the
child's good fortune in being born into such a magical family. There are
hopes that with this good pedigree he will grow into a man of spiritual
and magical power. As the event comes to a close and we begin to walk
toward our cars, the high priestess of a local coven comments on the
growing number of children being born in the community. Quoting from
the Bible that she read as a youth in a traditional Christian church, she
remarks: "To the tribe let there be children born that it might be mighty."

Background

The phenomenon of well-educated, middle-class Americans worshipping ancient deities, practicing magic, and participating in rites such as the one described in the prologue to this book has drawn the attention of both the media and a small body of academics. The Witchcraft movement is in many ways elusive, as there is no central bureaucracy or leader to determine orthodoxy. To the contrary, individual inspiration is encouraged. It is these very characteristics that have led some scholars (Luhrmann 1989; Ben-Yehuda 1985; Neitz 1991, 1994) to view Witchcraft as a cultural phenomenon or quasi-religion. I argue, following Beckford's (1984, 1992a, 1992b) model, that Witchcraft *is* a religion, and one that is particularly suited to the conditions of late modernity. Wicca, as its participants call it, like most new religions that developed in the 1960s, is aging. Very little research has been done on the process of maturation of new religious movements. However, this book will show that Wicca provides one model for the aging of new religious movements in late modernity.

BUT IS IT A RELIGION?

Among sociologists of religion, substantive and functional definitions have traditionally been used to distinguish religion and religious practices from the secular world. McGuire succinctly states, "Substantive definitions try to establish what religion is; functional definitions describe what religion does" (1992:10). Substantive definitions, such as those presented by P. Berger (1967) or Yinger (1970), focus on religions as social institutions that mediate the individual's relationship with the supernatural or sacred. As these definitions use Western religions as their model, they fit most closely with the intuitive view of religion held by most people in the United States. Functionalists define religions as social institutions that foster the creation of meaning. This latter definition would permit the inclusion of many different types of organizations, from Buddhism to Alcoholics Anonymous. Both definitions share a notion of religion as an organized social institution.

Some Witches, most particularly participants in all-women's groups, contend that they are participating not in a religion but in a spiritual path. They consider this distinction important because they view religions as oppressive organizations. They celebrate the fact that their practices and beliefs are not institutionalized. These participants, without necessarily being aware of it, accept the traditional sociological definitions of religion and therefore reject the term *religion*. The usefulness of each of these definitions, however, has come into question. McGuire (1992) suggests that they be considered strategies rather than truths. Greil and Robbins (1994) counsel that we view "religion as a category of discourse" (10). Barker (1994) contends that all definitions of religion are political in nature, as they affect which groups will be given benefits such as tax-deferred status and the ability to perform legal marriages.

Beckford (1984, 1992a, 1992b) asserts that the new religious and spiritual movements of late modernity challenge the traditional definitions of religion. Although Wicca is not specifically mentioned by Beckford, it does fit the model of New Age religions that he is analyzing. Beckford believes all of these religions share a holistic world image—that is, one in which the whole and the parts are enmeshed in a reciprocal relationship. Within these religions the individual is viewed as part of nature, not separate from it. Individual growth is simultaneously regarded as connected to cosmic changes and as helping to usher in those changes. The development and transformation of the self are therefore perceived as part of a process of social change. As there is an erosion between the personal and the political, the development of the self is viewed as part of the process of effecting necessary changes in the larger world, as well as in individuals' lives.

According to Beckford (1992b) these religions have components that would make them appear to reflect a postmodern sensibility. Most notably he refers to their playfulness, their rejection of instrumental rationality, and their pastiches of different traditions. Orion (1995), without substantiating it, claims that Wicca is a postmodern religion. Raphael (1996) contends that goddess spirituality has several components of a postmodern religion—in particular, "its eclectic, non-credal, laissez-faire thealogy" (200).[1] Nonetheless, she argues that goddess spirituality is a religion of late modernity and not of postmodernity. Referring to Eilberg-Schwartz (1989), Raphael asserts that the goddess movement is firmly entrenched within the Enlightenment tradition "as it turns the Enlightenment critique of religion against the Enlightenment's quasi-religious cult of Reason" (204).

Wicca, like the other religions that Beckford refers to and the women's-only spirituality groups that Raphael and Eilberg-Schwartz discuss, is a religion of late modernity rather than postmodernity. Although all of these religions have components of postmodernity, they do not ultimately signify an epistemological break with Enlightenment thought. Whether Wicca is a religion of postmodernity or late modernity may appear to be inconsequential; however, the distinction is important for placing the religion within its social and historical context. Postmodern theory brings all truth and moral claims into question and eliminates the active subject. As will be shown in this book, Wicca, while questioning moral issues, is part of the process in late modernity of reembedding moral issues through lifestyle choices. Ritual practices, community activities, and spiritual quests help to define lifestyle choices and are part of the creation and re-creation of the self within Wicca. The emphasis on globalism, the belief in personal and social transformation, and the use of noninstrumental rationality place Wicca firmly within the Enlightenment tradition.

THEORY

This book is informed both by Giddens's (1984, 1987, 1990, 1991) structuration theory and the work of scholars of new religious movements, such as Beckford. Although Giddens does not specifically discuss the role of religion, structuration theory provides a framework for understanding Wicca within the context of late modernity. Giddens argues both with and against postmodernist theorists.[2] According to Giddens, many of the claims of postmodernism—such as the death of the grand narrative, the questioning of truth claims, and the decentering of the subject—are not the result of the development of a new postmodern era, but rather are the logical outgrowth of Enlightenment rationality and science. Most notably, methodological doubt and the reflectivity of knowledge that are embedded in the tenets of science result in skepticism toward all knowledge claims. It is this skepticism that I will argue makes the practice of magic among even scientifically educated Witches seem both reasonable and appropriate.

In common with postmodern theorists, Giddens has been influenced by the linguistic turn in social science, according to which all knowledge is mediated through language. Truth is not viewed as something that can merely be searched for "out there"; rather, it must be understood as constructed through linguistic categories. Postmodernists contend that knowledge is at best fragmented and locally constituted through linguistic communities. The most radical of the postmodernists would assert that at most we can produce competing stories or narratives, each of which is equally justified, as there is no reality outside the signs and significations of language (Rosenau 1992).

Grand narratives, whether those of Marxism, evolutionary theory, or notions of progress, are all similarly viewed as suspect within postmodernist theory. As all truth claims are questioned, so are those of history, which claims to present overarching historical trends. Giddens argues that while methodological doubt is the norm within high modernity, this does not mean that all knowledge claims are equal. He suggests, for instance, that while no overall pattern can be determined in history, a disruption between traditional and modern societies can be discerned. The similarities in traditional societies and modernity are overshadowed by the distinctions between them. Modernity distinguishes itself by the speed with which change occurs, as well as by the far-reaching consequences of change. Within modernity, social institutions, expert systems, and symbolic tokens all become removed from immediate social relationships and their local context. Time and space are no longer connected to a particular location or set of activities, but they become universalized with global time zones, calendars, and maps. Similarly, symbolic tokens such as money become universalized. Expert systems, such as medicine, psychology, or mechanics, also become ubiquitous and outside of the immediacy of human relations. It is the disembedding of symbolic systems from time and space that provides the context in which Witches can borrow rituals, deities, and magical practices from around the globe. Within Wicca, spirituality as well as magic become expert systems that can be disembedded from a particular historical time or place. As will be shown in this book the routinization that is being experienced in Wicca is also an outgrowth of the development of expert systems.

Although Giddens, like the postmodernists, accepts the notion of the decentering of the subject, human agency remains an important category of inquiry for him. He does "not accept that this implies the evaporation of subjectivity into an empty universe of signs. Rather, social practices, biting into space and time, are considered to be at the root of the constitution of both subject and social object" (Giddens 1984:xxii). Giddens argues there is a dialectic between the individual as agent and the larger social structure. All information is mediated, through language and cultural symbols. Nonetheless, individuals actively participate in the construction of their lives, through the process of interpretation and through lifestyle choices. As tradition recedes as an organizing principle, people are forced to define themselves in ways that were not previously available. The process of self-definition is always in part determined by social factors, such as class, race, and gender. Within those limitations, however, people participate in the creation of self. Witches help to define themselves both by the very act of becoming a Witch and through the self-conscious use of rituals to create a persona. The Neo-Pagan community is one based on a lifestyle choice.

According to Giddens the political element of life choices is life politics. He differentiates between emancipatory politics and life politics. Emancipatory politics is "the effort to shed the shackles of the past ... [and] overcome the illegitimate domination of some individuals or groups by others" (Giddens 1991:211). On the other hand, life politics is the politics of choice—the choice to enter into and maintain an egalitarian relationship, the choice to act in a nonracist manner, the choice to be ecologically responsible, the choice to join organizations to ensure that your concerns with equity, the environment, or other issues are embedded within the society. As the slogan of the second wave of the women's movement suggested, "the personal is political." Giddens furthermore contends that through life politics "repressed existential issues, related not just to nature but to the moral parameter of existence as such, press themselves back on the agenda" (Giddens 1991:224). For Witches, whose religion embraces both feminism and ecological concerns, "the spiritual is political." Although Witches would contend that the only law is the Wiccan Rede—"do as thou will as long as thou harm none"—their very emphasis on women's issues, gay and lesbian issues, ecological issues, and respect for diversity are a call for the reembedding of social concerns within a moral framework.

NEO-PAGANISM AND WITCHCRAFT

Most of the adherents of Witchcraft are white, middle class, and well educated. In "The Pagan Census" we found that 90.4 percent of the respondents were white, 0.5 percent African American, 2 percent Asian, 9 percent Native American,[3] 0.8 percent Hispanic. Listing themselves as other were 2.2 percent and 5 percent did not respond. Only 7.6 percent claimed to have less than some college; 65.4 percent had at least a college degree; and 16.1 percent had completed postgraduate degrees (H. Berger et al. n.d.). Kirkpatrick et al. (1986) and Orion (1995) had similar findings. Because of the secrecy of participants, it is impossible to know the exact number of Neo-Pagans and Witches in the United States. Aidan Kelly extrapolates from mailing lists, festival attendance, and the number of covens in the area he knows best—the San Francisco Bay area—and estimates that there are 300,000 Neo-Pagans in the United States (1992:139–41). This is probably an over-estimation, as in each of the three methods he uses, Kelly is gauging the number of covens in the United States and multiplying the number of covens by ten, which he believes is the average coven membership. Ten members is plausibly the typical size of a coven, but it is probably not the average size, since there are probably more covens with a membership of less than ten than a membership of more than ten. Furthermore, although Kelly's estimate of covens seems well based on mailing lists and festival attendance, his third method, which uses the per capita number of covens in San Francisco as a template for the nation, brings his figures into question. While San Francisco is not unique it does have a higher ratio of Neo-Pagans than many other areas in the United States. However, since he does not include those individuals who practice alone or with one partner, his estimate is probably not as much of an over-approximation as it might at first appear. Even with the imperfections in his methods, Kelly provides the most reliable estimate to date, as he uses a combination of methods to arrive at his figure. If his estimate is cut by one-third to one-half, a more conservative number of 150,000 to 200,000 Neo-Pagans in the United States is reached.

As can be seen in the table below, Neo-Pagans live throughout the United States, with the largest percentage of adherents on the East and West Coasts. Most Neo-Pagans live in urban or suburban areas. In "The Pagan Census" only 15.8 percent of the respondents stated that they live in a rural area. In comparison, 27.9 percent noted living in a metropolitan area, 22.8 percent in a suburban area, 14.4 percent in a large town, 14.5 percent in small town, and 5.6 percent did not answer this question (H. Berger et al. n.d.).

Individuals come to the religion through several avenues. Some people learn about the religion through friends, others through reading a book or article about Neo-Paganism or Witchcraft, or by attending a class at an adult education center or occult bookstore. Adherents frequently assert that when they first encounter information about Neo-Paganism or Witchcraft they have a sense of "returning home." Neo-Pagans do not on the whole proselytize because they believe that each individual must find his or her own path to spiritual understanding (Adler 1979, 1986).

Distribution of Neo-Pagans Participating in Neo-Pagan Census in the U.S.

	n	%		n	%
Alabama	15	0.6	Nebraska	4	0.2
Alaska	2	0.1	Nevada	13	0.5
Arizona	44	1.8	New Hampshire	17	0.7
Arkansas	5	0.2	New Jersey	49	2.0
California	382	15.7	New Mexico	36	1.5
Colorado	49	2.0	New York	117	7.3
Connecticut	52	2.1	North Carolina	41	1.7
Delaware	9	0.4	North Dakota	2	0.1
Florida	89	3.7	Ohio	106	4.4
Georgia	68	2.8	Oklahoma	24	1.0
Hawaii	5	0.2	Oregon	48	2.0
Idaho	5	0.2	Pennsylvania	59	2.4
Illinois	90	3.7	Rhode Island	15	0.6
Indiana	25	1.0	South Carolina	20	0.8
Iowa	14	0.6	South Dakota	—	—
Kansas	21	0.9	Tennessee	1	0.1
Kentucky	16	0.7	Texas	14	0.6
Louisiana	4	0.2	Utah	112	4.6
Maine	18	0.7	Vermont	24	1.0
Maryland	69	2.8	Virginia	13	0.5
Massachusetts	184	7.6	Washington	65	2.7
Michigan	99	4.1	West Virginia	90	3.7
Minnesota	18	0.7	Wisconsin	7	0.3
Mississippi	5	0.2	Wyoming	35	1.4
Missouri	30	1.2	Wash., D.C.	1	0.1
Montana	7	0.3	Puerto Rico	8	0.3

Note: This table is based on responses to "The Pagan Census." As the distribution, as discussed in the preface, was not random, the actual percentages by state are at best an approximation.

Witchcraft is part of the larger Neo-Pagan movement. The distinction between the two is hard to define, but on the whole Witches are the more committed members of the religion. Adherents' self-definition as either a Witch or a Neo-Pagan is regularly accepted by others in the religion. Andras Corban Arthen suggested to me that "Neo-Pagans are just

Witches who haven't come out of the broom closet yet" (Andras Arthen Interview 1986). Most Neo-Pagans, however, take the label of Witch (Neitz 1991; Orion 1995). It is a label that brings with it many negative associations. As Arachne, the high priestess of the Circle of Light coven, revealed, "I hate the word; it has so many negative connotations. It is just loaded with negativity. I just don't want to present myself to the world that way" (Arachne Interview 1987). Both Arachne and others, however, do choose to define themselves as Witches. It may indeed be because of the negative implications of the term *Witch* that many individuals begin by calling themselves Pagans or Neo-Pagans and only as they become more involved in the religion take the label *Witch*.

Within Neo-Pagan circles the term *Witch* is viewed as an accolade, which describes an individual of power. The derivation of the term that is commonly presented by Witches is that it stems from the Old English word *Wik*, to bend or to shape. Witches are therefore individuals who have learned the craft of bending or shaping reality. The terms *Wicca*, *Wicce*, and *Wiccan* are believed to be the Middle English derivation of the term *Wik* (Arthen 1987; Adler 1979, 1986; Neitz 1991; Orion 1995).[4] Magic is part of the process through which Witches participate in reshaping their reality. Witches do not worship Satan, who as they note is a creation of Christianity.[5]

GERALD GARDNER

Witchcraft as it is practiced today in both England and the United States was strongly influenced by Gerald Gardner, an English civil servant. Gardner claimed to have been initiated in the 1930s by an old woman, Dorothy, who he asserted was a member of a coven that had survived and maintained its traditions through both the spread of Christianity and the English witch trials of the early modern period. After the repeal in 1951 of the English statutes against witchcraft, Gardner published two books describing what he maintained he learned from Old Dorothy (Adler 1979:62). Wicca, as Gardner presented it, is a gentle nature religion, in which the goddess of fertility and the horned god are venerated. There are eight sabbats throughout the year that correspond to the ancient agricultural festivals. Rituals are used both to celebrate the sabbats and to "raise energy" for magical workings. According to Gardner, Witches are able to project energy from their bodies, through dance, song, meditation, and directed thought that can be used to perform magical acts (Adler 1979, 1986; Neitz 1991; Orion 1995). The basic components of Wicca as presented by Gardner are practiced by most Neo-Pagan groups.

There is a debate within Witchcraft circles about the authenticity of Gardner's initiation. Valiente, one of the original members of Gardner's coven, is the strongest supporter of the veracity of Gardner's claim to have been initiated by Old Dorothy. She is not alone—Orion, an anthropologist who became a Witch during her research, is representative of a portion of the Neo-Pagan community that accepts Gardner's claims as true. Another anthropologist, Luhrmann, who during her research on British magical practitioners trained with Gardner's coven, also believes that Dorothy did initiate Gardner. However, Luhrmann doubts that Dorothy was a member of a group that existed prior to 1921, when Margaret Murray's first book—which argues that the individuals who were persecuted as witches in the early modern period were actually practitioners of an older pre-Christian religion—was published (Luhrmann 1989:43).

Most scholars (Neitz 1991; Kelly 1992) and many Neo-Pagans (Adler 1979, 1986; Bonewits 1989) discount Gardner's claims of having been initiated into a religion that had existed for several thousand years. However, this does not minimize his role in creating a coherent religious practice based in part on several different sources and his own inspiration. Regardless of their beliefs concerning the authenticity of Gardner's conversion, or the existence of covens that remained intact since the Middle Ages, adherents characterize their religion as a return to or restoration of the "old" pre-Christian pan-European faith, in which the earth is revered and the world is viewed as enchanted.

WICCA IN THE UNITED STATES

Raymond Buckland, a student of Gardner, is credited with introducing Wicca in the United States (Kelly 1992). Since migrating in the 1960s, Witchcraft has grown and taken a particularly American flavor. Mysticism, ecological concerns, women's rights, and anti-authoritarianism have all been incorporated into this new religion. Wicca in the United States is more eclectic than the religion in present day Great Britain (Orion 1995).

An elective affinity developed between Neo-Paganism and fantasy groups, the Society for Creative Anachronism, and science fiction groups (Ben-Yehuda 1985; Neitz 1991).[6] All these groups share a common interest in envisioning a different society than the present-day United States, in either the past, the future, or another galaxy. The influence of these groups is most clearly seen at festivals and gatherings where hundreds of Neo-Pagans come together. Intermingled with people in tie-dyed T-shirts and jeans are men and women dressed in medieval-style garb. Some groups refer to their members—and in fact all people they encounter in Neo-Pagan circles—as lord or lady. Both fantasy and science fiction literature and movies are very popular among Neo-Pagans. Some adherents initially learn about Neo-Paganism through their involvement in fantasy and science fiction groups (Neitz 1991).

Witchcraft and Neo-Paganism, as they have developed in the United States, have no central bureaucracy that can determine either dogma or orthodoxy. The lack of a central bureaucracy or dogma has resulted in the development of many branches or "traditions" within Witchcraft and Neo-Paganism.[7] It is possible for someone to develop her or his own idiosyncratic version of Neo-Paganism; however, there is a good deal of consistency among groups and individual practitioners. This consistency is in part due to the sharing of information at festivals, through computer networks, in journals, and in books. Neo-Pagans support more than one hundred journals and newsletters, in which information about rituals, practices, and ethics are shared and debated (H. Berger et al. n.d.). Although differences remain among groups, the major division within the religion is between all-women's and inclusive groups.[8] All-women's groups worship the goddess(es) to the exclusion of the god(s). These groups tend to be nonhierarchical, with the position of high priestess rotating among members. Inclusive groups, on the other hand, are composed of both heterosexual and homosexual men and women who venerate both the goddess(es) and the god(s). As instituted by Gardner, these groups usually have three ranks indicating different levels of knowledge and training. This book will focus on inclusive groups.

All-women's groups, which grew out of Wicca have been influenced by the feminist movement (Neitz 1991:355; Finley 1991). Some women who have joined the women's spirituality movement in fact were surprised to learn that many of the rites and rituals in which they participate originated in the Neo-Pagan movement (Finley 1991). The feminist spirituality movement, which views more traditional religions as patriarchal, focuses on the goddess as a symbol of women's lived experiences.

Finley (1991) and Neitz (1991) both contend that all-women's groups, unlike inclusive groups, offer the possibility of cultural or social change through the use of the goddess image. Finley believes that the all-women's groups will eventually disintegrate because of the lack of organizational structure. However, both Finley and Neitz suggest that the impact of the women's spirituality movement will continue to be felt, even if Neo-Paganism breaks apart. Although I agree with Finley that the sociological data would suggest that all-women's Witchcraft will eventually disintegrate, I believe this is not true for Witchcraft that is inclusive of women and men. It is the basic differences between all-women's and inclusive groups that I believe make the latter more likely to survive.

Although both types of Witchcraft are anti-authoritarian, inclusive groups from their inception have had some hierarchical elements. For instance, as previously mentioned, inclusive groups usually have within the covens three degrees or ranks, which signify levels of knowledge and accomplishment. Hence these Witchcraft groups have some elements that would allow the development of organizations that would ensure the continuance of the religion. Furthermore, inclusive groups involve entire families. Within all-women's groups, participants' husbands, male lovers, and sons are frequently excluded from participation in rituals. At one all-women's group that I visited, two of the participants spoke of their husbands' supporting their spiritual search. One noted that her husband was caring for their children while she was attending the ritual. Another woman, however, said that it took some negotiation with her husband to have him care for their children while she participated in a weekend workshop. She felt he was less supportive than her friend's husband of spiritual retreats. In either case, the practice of Witchcraft is not being integrated into the everyday life of these women and their families. Within Neo-Paganism there is a large representation of both homosexual women and men. Some all-women's groups are composed completely of lesbians or bisexual women.[9] While these women may include their female lovers in their religion, their sons' participation would be, at best, peripheral.

Contrary to Neitz (1991) and Finley (1991), I believe that inclusive groups within Witchcraft will ultimately prove to be more significant. Inclusive groups, like all-women's groups, are also influenced by feminism. Although Gardner and some of the early groups that grew out of his original coven incorporated traditional gender roles, Wicca in the United States, particularly among newer groups and younger participants, emphasizes feminist ideals. Most of the female participants were drawn to the religion because they viewed it as a feminist form of spirituality. By involving men, inclusive groups also provide a "social laboratory" (Robbins and Bromley 1992) for alternative gender roles of both men and women.

Possibly more importantly, inclusive groups are more likely to include and fully involve children in their practices. It is the birth of children into the Neo-Pagan community that I believe will have the greatest impact on this new religion. In "The Pagan Census" we found that 41.3 percent of all participants stated that they have children, with only 0.02

percent not responding to this question (H. Berger et al. n.d.). I have witnessed that a growing number of children are being born within the New England Neo-Pagan community. This is not surprising, as many of the participants who entered the religion in their twenties are now in their thirties and forties. Children wiccaned into the faith will be maintainers of their families' practice, instead of neophytes of a new religion.

Witchcraft, as was noted at the beginning of this chapter, is different from many mainline religions and other new religions. Both Marty (1970) and Truzzi (1972) have contended that modern occultists, including Witches, are not participating in a serious religion, but a leisure-time activity. I have heard similar comments from people I have spoken to about my research. I think this misconception of Witchcraft in part grows from the emphasis in the research on all-women's groups, particularly those groups composed mostly of heterosexual women, who separate their spiritual quests from other aspects of their lives. For some social scientists, furthermore, the belief and practice of magic among educated middle-class people is viewed as at best an oddity and not a serious religious expression.

Witches' involvement in their religion can vary greatly. While many Witches are initiated through a training program that lasts from a year and a day to several years, some people have become Witches by declaring themselves as such. One woman told me she was initiated by the goddess. The boundaries of this religion are permeable, with some people only marginally involved. They come to rituals or to retreats for fun, in the hope of finding a sexual partner, or because they have a friend who is going. Enjoying the people they meet or finding a lover results in their returning to other events. They may take the label Witch or Neo-Pagan or not. Some of these people, after staying at the periphery for a few years, leave the Neo-Pagan community, returning to more mainline religions, secularism, or another new religious movement. Others start to become more involved; they may begin seriously reading about Witchcraft, join a coven, or take a course offered at an occult bookstore or an adult education center, such as the one offered by Andras Corban Arthen at the Cambridge Adult Education Center. Although for those individuals who are only peripherally involved Witchcraft may be a "leisure-time" activity, this is not true for the committed, many of whom place their religious commitment above career. It is these individuals who are central to the religion, and whose time and energy goes into organizing covens, organizations, journals, newsletters, and festivals. In this respect Wicca resembles more mainline religions, which also have members with differing levels of involvement.

RITUALS

Witchcraft is a mystery religion, in which rituals take precedence over any particular set of beliefs (Neitz 1991:356). Witches participate in four different types of rituals: sabbats, esabats, rites of passage, and personal rituals. The basic elements of rituals, the casting of the circle, the calling of the four quarters, the sharing of cakes and wine, and the unwinding of the circle at the end of the ritual were initially presented by Gerald Gardner. The specific details—which gods and goddesses are invoked or which actual words are used in casting the circle—vary from group to group in the United States. It is the myth of a unified ancient pagan tradition that permits Neo-Pagans to self-consciously combine aspects of pre-Judeo-Christian religions and modern non-Western religions with individual inspiration. Witches frequently speak of returning to a pagan celebration of life and of nature.[10] While some groups focus on a particular tradition—for instance, Egyptian, Celtic, or Native American— most combine several traditions. The gods and goddesses of different pantheons are viewed as different manifestations of the same forces. Neo-Pagans search for information about pre-Judeo-Christian religious practices. While some aspects of these religions are rejected, such as the subjugation of women or the use of human sacrifices, other aspects are used to create new rituals and practices. In all cases the practices of ancient cultures are disembedded from the original social relationships in which they grew.

The underlying link for Neo-Pagans among these divergent religions is their reverence for nature. Not surprisingly, the worship of nature is central to Neo-Paganism. Both the cycle of the seasons and the moon phases are celebrated. The eight yearly sabbats commemorate the beginning and height of each season. Ostava, which most Neo-Pagans consider the New Year, occurs on the vernal equinox, March 21, the beginning of spring. Paralleling the changes in nature, this is seen as a time of new beginnings for people, a time during which old ties are renewed and new ones established. At the Ostava rituals, chocolate rabbits and dyed eggs are traditionally distributed as symbols of fertility—fertility of thoughts and actions, even more than fertility of crops and animals. There is on the whole a deemphasis on human fertility. At a recent Ostava ritual I attended, energy was raised for the purpose of increasing the fertility of endangered species, such as whales. Neo-Pagans note that the symbols of eggs and rabbits were taken over by Christianity when it was a new religion. According to the high priestess and priest of the Circle of Light coven, historically the eggs were painted with pictures or symbolic representations of things that were desired for the coming year and then placed in the earth as a seed to grow. At every Ostava ritual I have attended the participants plant seeds to symbolize their wishes for the coming year.

Beltane, or May Day (May 1), is the celebration of the height of spring and emphasizes the continuation of fertility and growth that began this season. The traditional dance around the maypole is a celebration of the fertility of the season. This dance symbolizes the sex act, as men and women holding brightly colored ribbons weave in and out. The maypole is envisaged as a phallic symbol that is placed in a hole in the mother earth. The magic performed at this time of year has alternatively been explained to me at different Beltane celebrations as either symbolically capturing the sun in the woven ribbons, or weaving the participants' wishes into the pole, a form of string magic. The rituals that take place during this time commemorate the regeneration of both the female element, as represented in the mother earth, and the birth from the mother of her son, the Sun King. This is the time of the renewal of the earth and the growing strength of the sun. Sexuality—heterosexual, homosexual, and bisexual— is openly celebrated at Neo-Pagan rituals. Sex is seen as a magically powerful act.

As the wheel of the seasons turns, so do the holidays. The summer begins on the longest day of the year, June 21. During this holiday, the sun, now at full strength, is celebrated, but so is the beginning of its descent into winter. While this is a joyous holiday, there is a remembrance that the sun now at its height will start waning. Lammas, which takes place on August 1, commemorates the height of summer and is the first harvest celebration. Just as the beginning of life is commemorated in the spring, so in the fall, death is celebrated. This is not a glorification of death, but a coming to terms with one's own as well as nature's cycle of death. Many, although not all, Neo-Pagans believe in reincarnation and hence see each life as just one in a cycle. Life and death are seen as interdependent aspects or parts of one whole, as all life is dependent on death. Plants and animals are killed as food in order for life to continue. New life finds room on the planet only because the old and worn die.

Although the commemoration of death is foreshadowed in the summer, it is at the autumn equinox that the celebration of death begins. This period reaches its climax with Samhain or what would commonly be called Halloween. Samhain is a time when the veil between the worlds of the living and the dead is deemed to be at its weakest. It is believed that spirits can, therefore, more readily be felt on earth. The season of death, winter, is commemorated by a celebration of the return of life. Yule celebrations, which occur on December 21, the shortest day of the year, emphasize that the worst of winter is soon to pass. The sun is again increasing in strength. At the one Yule celebration I attended, the participants were asked to wear gold or silver clothing. People dressed in various outfits, ranging from a golden gown worn by a woman who had bought it secondhand after last year's proms were over, to sparkles on the faces or in the hair of others. The ritual itself emphasized joyousness and the growth in strength of the sun, which was in direct contrast to the darkness and cold of the outside world. A large representation of the sun was brought into the circle at one point in the ritual. Everyone then joined hands to dance in faster and faster circles around the sun, to commemorate the beginning of its ascent. Imbolc, or Candlemas, which is celebrated on February 2, is the height of winter. It is the ending of winter and the coming of the spring which is revered at this holiday, more than winter itself. Numerous candles are often lit at Imbolc rituals to denote the growing strength of the sun and the lengthening of daylight.

Besides the celebration of sabbats, the Neo-Pagans also celebrate the moon cycles: the full, new, and quarter moons. These celebration are known as esabats. The moon is seen as a feminine deity, which has three phases or faces—the maid, the mother, and the crone. Each is seen as having special powers. The esabats are, on one hand, like the sabbats—the celebration of the cycle of birth, growth, and death, although on a smaller scale, taking place within a twenty-eight-day period. On the other hand, they are also the celebration of the female aspect in all of us—that is, the nurturing, life-giving force. The moon, the female deity, in twenty-eight days goes through its cycle of birth, growth, death, and ultimately rebirth, just as in life women in that same approximate time span go from ovulation to either fertilization or menstruation and back to ovulation.

Rites of passage have been devised by Neo-Pagans to commemorate life events: birth, maturation into adulthood, marriage or the joining of two or more adults in a relationship, croning, and death. There are also personal rituals, which occur when individuals become initiated into Wicca, take a magical name, or participate in healing rites. All of these rituals connect the individual to a community of believers as well as commemorate a personal change within their lives.

MAGIC

Witches practice magic. Wishes, or spoken words particularly when part of a ritual done by those who have developed their magical skills, are believed to have a direct effect on the world. Magic is considered to be efficacious in solving a wide variety of problems, from finding an apartment or a lover to helping find a cure for AIDS. Magic, a force for either good or evil, is believed to work by tapping into the forces of nature. One can bring health to a friend or equally one could bring illness to a foe. Among Witches there are ethical sanctions against use of magic for harm, or even use of magic without the permission of those who could be affected by it. For example, it is considered unethical to send healing magic to an ill person who has not given his or her permission. Witches contend that the energy you send out will return to you threefold.[11] Therefore, individuals who do use magic for evil purposes have left themselves psychically open to harm.

Magic is based on a concept of the universe as an ordered web in which all events are interconnected and do not result solely from chance. The mind or individual will, when properly directed, is posited to affect the workings of the world. It is believed that we all perform magical acts, even if we are unaware of doing them. For instance, we think about someone intently, hoping to hear from them, only to have them get in contact with us. Witches contend that individuals differ in their ability to perform magic. The analogy I have heard from many different sources is that of learning to play the piano. Almost everyone can learn to play the piano, although some people have more native ability than others. However, if even the most talented person is not introduced to the instrument, his or her abilities will never be discerned, let alone developed. Analogously, it is the Witch's training that prepares her or him to perform magic. Some individuals are noted for being more magically powerful or gifted than others. More usually, particular Witches are known to be gifted in one aspect of magic, such as astral projection or reading tarot cards.

Magic is based on a concept of occult knowledge. Galbreath (1983) described occult or hidden knowledge as taking three forms:

(1) extraordinary matters that by virtue of their intrusion into the mundane world are thought to possess special significance (e.g. omens, portents, apparitions, prophetic dreams);
(2) matters such as the teaching of . . . mystery schools that are kept hidden from the uninitiated and unworthy;
(3) matters that are intrinsically hidden from ordinary cognition and understanding but nonetheless knowable through the awakening of hidden, latent faculties of appropriate sensitivity. (18–19)

Although Galbreath's distinction is helpful in differentiating occult phenomena, in practice the three categories overlap. This is particularly true for categories one and three. Part of a Witch's training is an increased sensitivity to acknowledging and interpreting omens and spirits and to seeing the extraordinary in everyday events. Through interaction with others in the community, the initiate is taught to reinterpret events. For example, when I participated in Andras Corban Arthen's class on Witch-craft at the Cambridge Adult Education Center, one woman stated that she had decided to take the class because it seemed interesting. After she became an initiated Witch, I heard her redefine why she had enrolled in the class. She stated that she had been drawn to the class because she knew it would provide her with information she was seeking. Her personal history was filtered through a magical worldview, in which all events would have meaning after she became an initiated Witch. Luhrmann refers to this as learning to speak "with a different rhythm" (1989). All life's events are reinterpreted so that things that might be ignored or viewed as a coincidence are perceived as an omen or a prophetic dream.

Mystery schools provide a stringent training in magic. The initiate is taught a number of techniques including astral projection, calling of spirits, and magical rites that will directly affect the course of events. The training teaches initiates both magical techniques and criteria for assessing the results. For instance, one Witch, a high priest who helps train the neophytes in his coven in ceremonial magic, once told me that he did a ritual during a drought to ensure rain. He knew it had worked when a water pipe broke in his basement, where he had done the ritual. He had brought rain, not to the earth from the sky, but down into his basement temple from the overhead pipes.

Luhrmann, in her study conducted in Great Britain, distinguishes between ceremonial magicians and Witches. She views the former as a more intellectual enterprise and the latter as an earthier, more intuitive form of magic (Luhrmann 1989:56). With the exception of all-women's groups, which tend to have a less formal, more intuitive form of magic, the distinction is less clear among U.S. groups than those described by Luhrmann. As Orion (1995) notes, "Wicca derives its ancestry not only from fertility cults but from the magico-religion of Egypt. . . . Finding the rituals in Old Dorothy's Book of Shadows fragmentary, Gardner wanted to enhance them to make them more workable. . . . For this purpose, Gardner resorted to the wealth of resources preserved in the Western occult tradition" (79). Orion presents a very detailed description of the Western magical tradition as most Witches, although not all, believe that it has developed. Orion in this instance is speaking more as a participant than a scholar. She contends that the Western magical tradition developed first in the Nile Valley during the Ptolemaic and Roman periods, when Egyptian and Roman magical traditions converged. This tradition, which was later influenced by the Gnostic scholars, subsequently found its way into the Byzantium empire, where it was further developed. During the Renaissance, the magical tradition was reintroduced to Europe, where it influenced the growing number of magicians (Orion 1995:80).

Orion provides a very clear and well-substantiated narrative of the flow of magical knowledge from classical sources to Renaissance writers and practitioners. She does not equally substantiate how the tradition was kept alive until Gardner integrated it with Old Dorothy's teachings. The actual ancestry of the Wiccan magical tradition appears to be more directly an outgrowth of nineteenth-century magical groups (Luhrmann 1989), most particularly the Hermetic Order of the Golden Dawn. The founders, who had been Freemasons, studied ancient texts, taking symbols from Greek and Egyptian sources, and claimed to have found an encoded Rosicrucian document.

ANTIQUITY

The notion of an unbroken magical tradition is another element of what Margot Adler refers to as the myth of Wiccan revival: "Witchcraft is a religion that dates back to paleolithic times, to the worship of the god of the hunt and the goddess of fertility. One can see remnants of it in cave paintings and in the figurines of goddesses that are many thousand years old. This early religion was universal. The names changed from place to place but the basic deities were the same" (Adler 1986:45). According to the myth, the religion died out slowly as the nobility and eventually the commoners were converted to Christianity. But pockets of the old religion remained intact, hidden in rural areas. The gods of the old religion were transformed into devils by the new religion, while the holidays of the old religion were incorporated into Christianity.

The essential elements of this myth are an outgrowth of the work of Margaret Murray ([1921] 1971, 1977) who first suggested that the witch trials of the early modern period were an attempt by the church to eliminate the remaining adherents of an earlier religion. Margaret Murray's research was initially well received but has lost credibility within academic circles (Trevor-Roper 1969; Rose 1962). Most of the Witches I know, influenced in part by Margot Adler, do not literally interpret the myth. However, I have spoken with others who believe that they are carrying on their families' tradition of Witchcraft and magic. The antiquity of practice, whether it is viewed as a re-creation or a return, is an important element of participants' perception of their own religious practice.

The view of Wicca as the "old religion" is important for four reasons. First, Witches want to differentiate themselves from other new religious movements, which they view as dominated by gurus. Linda, one of the original members of the Circle of Light coven, recounted reassuring her mother that she was not becoming involved in a "cult" by noting that "I am giving neither my will nor my money to another person." Second, Witches legitimate their religious practice by viewing it as old—their practices precede those of Judaism, Christianity, and Islam. Third, by viewing their religious practice within historical terms, they develop a shared past. The identification with historical Witches provides a period of martyrdom, similar to that which has been experienced by other Western religions, particularly Judaism. As Brad Hicks notes in a handout, "Some of the people that the Church burned as Witches were people who believed and practiced the same things that I do. In identification with them and the suffering that they went through some of us [Neo-Pagans] call ourselves Witches" (Hicks n.d.). The "burning times," as Witches refer to the period of the witch trials, provide a symbol to unite the community. Witches quote the number of people killed during the period of the trials and refer to it as their holocaust. They believe that they must be vigilant to forestall another one.

Fourth, Witches believe that their religious practice links them to an alternative worldview, one that provides a healthier attitude toward nature, oneself, and other people. As Joe, a Neo-Pagan in his twenties, phrased it, "If we hadn't left behind that respect for earth, that respect for each other, we would not have nuclear weapons—no one would blow up an earth they consider sacred—they just won't" (Joe Interview 1988). Neo-Pagans maintain that pre-Christian communities lived in balance with nature because they revered it, seeing it as a manifestation of the goddess. Similarly, the worship in old Pagan communities of goddesses as well as gods is believed to have resulted in women being considered equal, if not superior, to men. Ron, a man in his early fifties and a Witch for more than twenty years, claimed, "It is very hard to have a belief system where you have as one deity a goddess and [at the same time] be nasty to women" (Ron Interview 1986).

Women's spirituality groups present a more radical portrait of this mythical past. Prehistoric societies are viewed within these groups as having worshiped the goddess to the exclusion of any male deities. These societies are depicted as matriarchies in which women were seen as the natural leaders and the centers of peaceful, cooperative, emotionally supportive, and ecologically healthy communities (Eller 1993:157–62).

MAGIC AND SCIENCE

Based in part on the works of scholars (Murray [1921] 1971, 1977; Keller 1985; Merchant 1980; Ehrenreich and English 1973), Neo-Pagans have come to frame their understanding of the breakdown of the older world order, in which the world was viewed as enchanted, as the result of the development of a patriarchal, rationalist worldview. The people, primarily women, executed in the witch craze are believed to be martyrs to the growth of the new world order. They are viewed as having been healers, wisewomen, and/or maintainers of the "old ways."

Starhawk (1982), a Witch who is widely read within Neo-Pagan circles, contends that the Witch craze of the early modern time was central in the transition to a new world order.[12] Her analysis is well referenced and substantially supported by scholarly research. She contends that "During the sixteenth and seventeenth centuries, Western society was undergoing massive changes. . . . As part of that change, the persecution of the Witches was linked to three interwoven processes: the expropriation of land and natural resources; the expropriation of knowledge; and the war against the consciousness of immanence, which was embodied in women, sexuality and magic" (Starhawk 1982:189). The trials ended, Starhawk notes, with the acceptance of mechanical philosophy, the forerunner of modern science. Matter was seen as devoid of animism, and the world became disenchanted. The notion of the devil or spirits being involved came to be viewed as absurd. Starhawk notes that the mechanical philosophers had by this time won their battle against the magicians or hermetic philosophers. The trials helped to discredit this alternative view of the universe as alive, animate, and interconnected. The worldview put forth by the mechanical philosophers was one that was based on the domination of nature and of women.

Starhawk claims, "Yet mechanism has, in the long run, proved invalid. Physicists now tell us that there are not solid atoms—only interactions among particles, which themselves may be patterns of probabilities, none of which can be observed objectively because observation requires interaction with the observed" (Starhawk 1982:217). Keller (1985), a scientist, similarly contends that the new physics may be ushering in a paradigm switch in science, one that in some ways reflects the worldview of the hermetic philosophers. The notion of magic's having historical roots in what some scholars consider an alternative scientific path is viewed by some Witches as a justification of their practices. Although looking back prior to the Enlightenment for the basis of their magical worldview, Witches are not rejecting the Enlightenment project. Instead, they are accepting its basic premise of skepticism. As Ariel, a graduate student in the sciences and a Witch, contends, "There is a narrow science view and the broader science view. There are some people—mostly people who don't know science that well—who treat it as a very religious thing. That anything that science hasn't sanctified must not exist. And they completely do not admit the existence of a wide range of everyday phenomena" (quoted in H. Berger 1994). Science is viewed as providing a view of reality, but as members of late modernity, Witches accept multiple realities. As John, another scientist who is a Witch, stated, "Physics is purely a theory—it is a model and a model is different from the thing which it describes—it is sheerly an approximation that has predictive power. Even if you have a perfect model there is no way that you can know it is perfect. So there is no reason you can't have two separate models for how thermodynamics works" (quoted in H. Berger 1994).

Witches in the United States take their magical teachings from a wide variety of sources—the recorded techniques of Egyptian or Renaissance ceremonial magicians, the teachings of shamans from many different cultures, meditation and other spiritual procedures from Eastern mysticism—all mixed together. The justification for this is that while these teachings come from different traditions, they all are concerned with similar types of experiences and knowledge. As Gabriel, the high priest of the Circle of Light coven, noted, "Magic can be done in a number of ways. There are a number or techniques to place yourself in an alternative consciousness in which you can assert your will" (Gabriel Interview 1987). Witches learn—through books, classes, and each other—techniques for astral projection, mediation, and spells. Some like Gabriel state that they rely on one basic form of magic; others claim to be eclectic. In either case magic becomes an abstract system of practices for Witches, disembedded from their culture(s) of origin.[13] The clearest example of this is presented by Bonewits in his book *Real Magic* (1989), in which he outlines "the laws of magic." I have been told repeatedly by Witches that they became convinced of magic by seeing it work. They claim that it is not a matter of faith but of empiricism. "If it works it's true" (Bonewits 1989:13–14).

"White Water was my first magical name, which I took when I and my High Priestess were first forming our coven. I had at that time felt myself to be like white water, full of energy and power but undirected. My coven has now been in existence for ten years, and six years ago I made a commitment to a woman, and more recently our child. My life has changed and this new name reflects that change."[1]

After Three Blade Jaguar speaks, Laima puts on a mask, transforming herself into a smiling goddess with black hair. She distributes masks to the other coven members. As each person puts on a mask, he or she takes on the persona of a deity. One mask is of the quarter moon, one of an unspecified animal, and another of a crone. Each coven member in turn comes forward to tell Three Blade Jaguar about the meaning of his new name. I can only half hear the speeches, as they are directed toward the center of the circle where Three Blade Jaguar stands and are spoken behind plastic masks in eerie, unnatural voices. However, through the fog of distorted speech I can hear the first woman, who wears the mask of the half moon, remind Three Blade Jaguar that he has dedicated his life to the goddess, and that his path is chosen. A man wearing the animal mask speaks of what the three blades represent. One is to protect his people, one is to protect his spirituality, and one is for the hunt, which the animal-masked man tells us is a man's mission. He further comments that White Water had been a young, single man who could seek his own pleasures, but Three Blade Jaguar is now a grown man with responsibilities. His son will one day take his place, but for now it is Three Blade Jaguar's responsibility to care for his family and his people.

As each coven member speaks, he or she tells of the changes that the new name represents. Each person after speaking removes the mask, revealing again the face and voice of a friend. We had gathered to witness this man taking a new name. As at the wiccaning, everyone brought a gift for the "new person" who entered the community. In this case the gifts were those most suited for an adult and a member of this community. He received a handmade cape, a new ritual robe, a pewter candlestick, ritual jewelry, and a box to store them in. This was an important ritual for him, because through taking a new name he both acknowledged and helped to foster a personal transfiguration.

Most of the literature on self-transformation within new religious movements has focused on healing rituals (Beckford 1984; Orion 1995) and specifically on women's healing rites (Eller 1993; Jacobs 1989, 1991). I want to extend this analysis to include both rituals that cannot directly be classified as involving healing and those that look at gendered rituals for men as well as women. Self-creation of men and women through ritual has certain similarities. In both instances, the ritual involves the creation of gendered selves. Furthermore, rituals of the self, whether gender neutral or for either women or men, share the adaptation of traditional societies' practices within a modern context.

SELF-IDENTITY

In modernity the self is negotiated and defined. The notion of one essential personality that is immutable is consistent with community life based on face-to-face interactions (Gergen 1991). In these societies tradition and dogma are significant determinants of the circumscribed parameters that define people's relationship with their society. Consistency of character is prized. Although tradition—particularly as it is formalized in routine—continues to play an important part in people's lives within modernity, it is open to scrutiny of abstract systems of thought, such as medical, psychological, economic, and sociological discourses. All people are influenced by these abstract systems, which are mediated for the lay person through the media, intermediaries, or selected interactions with professionals. As Giddens suggests, "Self-identity today is a reflexive achievement. The narrative of self-identity has to be shaped, altered and reflexively sustained in relation to rapidly changing circumstances of social life, on a local and global scale. The individual must integrate information deriving from a diversity of mediated experiences with local involvement in such a way as to connect future projects with past experiences in a reasonably coherent fashion" (1991:215).

A Promethean self is encouraged in modernity, as it permits the individual to survive and flourish in changing circumstances (Gergen 1991). Therapeutic movements are part of the process through which individuals reflectively contemplate the creation of self-identity and learn to minimize the risks inherent in modern society (Giddens 1990, 1991). The abstract systems of psychology, psychoanalysis, or more eclectic forms of therapy have become enmeshed in the practices of many new religious movements (Beckford 1984; Hervieu-Leger 1990; McGuire 1994). These religions offer their participants practices whose aim is the transfiguration of the self.

Beckford, responding to critics who have suggested that the emphasis on self-transformation within these new religious movements is promulgating narcissism,[2] contends to the contrary that these religions "tend to support a crucial part of the middle class value system, namely the belief that people should be trained for specific professional roles. The idea that people display an immutable character or a fixed set of capacities is entirely discredited in the culture at large as well as in NRHMs [New Religious and Healing Movements]" (Beckford 1984:267). It is the self-transformative elements of these new religions that Beckford believes make them "social vehicles of the sacred in the present-day world" (259).

Although many of the rituals in Wicca have elements of healing, this is not universally the case. The naming ritual described at the beginning of this chapter is a good example of a ritual of self-transformation that is not limited to healing. However, these rituals do have a therapeutic component that focuses on the transformation of self-identity. Judy,[3] the high priestess of a New York coven, suggested,

> Ritual is among other things a psychological technology. . . . Sigmund Freud said dreams are the royal road to the unconscious. He was only partially right—it is a two-way road. Dreams may be the royal road from the unconscious or one of them. But there are royal roads to the unconscious. When we don't just want to hear what the unconscious is saying, when we want to do something with it we want to change something down deep in there, and ritual is about that. (Judy Interview 1987)

Within the Neo-Pagan community, rituals are simultaneously viewed as having a psychological and a mystical component. These are not seen as antithetical to one another; they may in fact be viewed as complementary. Rituals are in part organized around changing the self, in relationship to changes that are occurring in the individual's life trajectory and in terms of changes within the larger society.

RITUAL OF THE SELF

Sabbats are, primarily, celebrations of the changing seasons, compelling all those who participate to become aware of the fluctuations in the natural world. In each of these celebrations a parallel is drawn between changes in the natural world and those in each participant's personal life. In 1989 I attended an open Samhain ritual held in a room rented from a local Unitarian Universalist church. The ritual was organized by EarthSpirit Community, which is noted for its very dramatic presentations that accommodate and involve large groups. About eighty to one hundred people participated in this ritual. They were drawn from the membership of EarthSpirit, the larger Neo-Pagan community, and interested outsiders who had seen the announcement of the event or been invited by a friend. As I looked around the crowd I recognized the majority of people by sight if not by name. There were a few outsiders, including four of my students who had accompanied me.

The room was softly lit, with a circle of four people in hooded black robes sitting facing the center. When I entered the room I thought I heard Gregorian chants, but once my ears had adjusted I realized that the four people in the center were humming in a mournful tone. At six spots throughout the room, figures in black hooded robes sat at one side of a circle created with autumn leaves, pine cones, and small candles. As people entered the room, they joined one of these groups. In the first group I joined, the hooded figure was speaking of his grandmother's death. People were encouraged to speak of the deaths of those close to them. One woman spoke of a friend's recent death from breast cancer. A man recounted his sense of helplessness as he watched his father die. Another man related his loss of a dear friend with whom he had lived for over a decade, revealing at the end of his story that the friend was his dog. In each circle people were speaking of deaths of family members, friends, and mentors. Some people cried as they spoke or heard about the losses of others. Everyone sitting in the circle appeared moved by their own memories and others' tales of loss.

After setting the tone for the ritual, the small circles dissolved into one large amoebic form around the edge of the room. The circle was cast, the four directions called, and the members of EarthSpirit enacted a short play in which death was depicted—as a friend as much as the grim reaper. During this ritual we were asked to call out the names of people who had passed on to the other realm and also to recall the joys we had experienced with them. A cacophony of names and experiences rang through the hall, making it impossible to decipher any one name or experience. Subsequently we were requested to reflect on the death of nature, of people, or of negative aspects of our lives. Death was portrayed as a time of new beginnings as well as of endings. We were led in a meditation in which we were invited to reflect on the aspects of our lives that we wanted to have die—things such as unhappiness or boredom. After we meditated on our lives, contemplated our death, and thought about our losses, the group was led in a spiral dance during which everyone chanted: "It is the blood of the ancestors that flows through our veins, the forms change but the circle of life remains."[4]

Some particulars of this Samhain ritual differed from others that I have attended, because each group is innovative in the creation of its rituals and because this was a large open ritual, which necessitates a different format than the smaller rituals I have attended at covens. However, all of the Samhain rituals have a certain similarity in that death and renewal are celebrated. In all cases there is a cathexis about death—the prospect of one's own death, the death of loved ones, and the death of aspects of one's personality.

At other sabbats, different aspects of nature and of the individual's life are celebrated. For instance, at Beltane, which occurs in the spring, the focus moves from death to birth. These rituals celebrate the renewal of nature, and focus on individuals planting the seeds of change or growth that they hope to harvest in the coming year. At several Beltane rituals I attended, we literally planted seeds, either directly into the earth or in small pots to bring home. These were living symbols of the budding of new life in nature and within the lives of the participants.

The ritual is expected to work for the person both by putting him or her in tune with the changing environment and by helping the person alter his or her own life. Individual transformations are viewed as functioning in three interrelated modes. First, there is an expectation that the energy raised within the ritual will help to bring to fruition one's wishes, whether for renewal, birth, change, or continuation. The dancing, singing, and group "energy" is believed to bring forth the will of the group and of the individuals within it. Second, the will of the goddess(es) and god(s) who were invoked adds to the power of the ritual and magical workings. Third, the ritual works by helping to focus the individual's knowledge and will on changes that she or he hopes to accomplish. The last of these three is the most psychological in orientation but all three focus on self-transformation.

MYSTICISM IN EVERYDAY LIFE

Within Wicca, one element of self-transformation is the acceptance of a mystical worldview. Luhrmann (1989) contends that modern practitioners of magic learn through their training to alter the way they perceive the world. According to Luhrmann, the alteration in perception is based on three basic changes in individuals' attitudes and behaviors. First, there is a change in how people analyze events. For instance, after a ritual, participants look for ways the ritual has worked and accept as evidence things that they might previously have conceived as coincidence. Second, people have moving experiences, such as being out of body, or having mood shifts through creative visualization or meditation. These events become an important part of their life experiences, which provide them with a new type of knowledge.

Third, magicians participate in deep play, in which they are able to act out visions of alternative worlds and alternative roles for themselves. These changes in perception affect how people view their own life trajectories and organize their life choices.

The goddess, or the powers within the universe, becomes an important part of Witches' lives. Witches do not believe in coincidences. The whole concept of coincidence has been developed, they suggest, to explain away mystical events that we all experience. Through understanding and attempting to solicit mystical or nonmundane experiences, Witches believe they can better organize and control their lives. Melanie, a graduate of the Massachusetts Institute of Technology (MIT), illustrates how magical activities become part of life planning. Melanie, who was in graduate school when I met her, confided that she had not gone directly to college after high school. She decided to apply to undergraduate programs after being told in a tarot reading that she should look for a teacher. Initially she had thought that she required a new spiritual teacher, but subsequently she was sent signs that she needed a teacher in the mundane world. She then did another reading to determine which of the offers from prestigious institutions she should accept. For Melanie the tarot readings were a sign from the goddess of the next step she needed to take in her life (Melanie Interview 1988).

Although there are elements of fatalism in this worldview, it is less a passive acceptance of fate than an active reshaping of the individual's life. Laurie Cabot[5] informed me that the reason to seek out knowledge about the future is to be able to reshape it (Laurie Cabot Interview 1989). Having a tarot reading, scrying, or other forms of soothsaying done for them, or doing it for themselves, are ways in which Witches attempt to control their destiny. Although the categories are not those of risk management, they are nonetheless concerned with control of the individual's destiny. Witches do tarot readings, but, like Melanie, they also apply to schools, take standardized examinations, and write application essays. The goddess is one way in which Witches organize and think about their lives.

The meaning of the goddess(es) or god(s) is not always clear within Wicca. The deities are called into the circle at all rituals. Most Witches also have altars to the deities, the goddess, or to a particular set of goddesses and/or gods in their home. Like Melanie, many Witches speak of receiving signs from the goddess or of trusting the goddess to guide them. The goddess is a more central and important image within Wicca than the god, even in those groups in which both are invoked. As one popular chant proclaims, "We all come from the goddess and to her we shall we return, like a drop of water running to the river." The goddess is wor-

PERSONAL TRANSFORMATIONS

Although all rituals involve an element of self-reflection and self-transformation, some rituals are directly geared toward the transformation of the self. The naming ritual is one example, but so are rituals of puberty and those of croning.[8] As Giddens notes, "Transitions in individuals' lives have always demanded psychic reorganization, something which was often ritualized in traditional cultures in the shape of *rites de passage*. . . . In the settings of modernity, by contrast the altered self has to be explored and constructed as part of a reflexive process of connecting personal and social change" (Giddens 1991:32–33). Wiccan rituals, as a particular form of reflectivity of self, have commonalities with rites of passage of traditional societies. This is not surprising as Witches use both historical and anthropological accounts of rituals to help create their own. Unlike traditional rites, however, present-day Wiccan rituals provide one form of "construction" of self in late modernity.

In traditional societies rituals are grounded within conventions of that culture, and rites of passage are socially determined. Although there may be differences in individual responses to the rite, the transformation is from one socially determined status to another (Turner 1969). For example, a girl who participates in a puberty rite is transfigured into a woman as that role is defined in her culture. Modern Wiccan rituals also serve as an avenue for transformation that is socially affirmed by other members of the Neo-Pagan community. However, the script for that metamorphosis, including how the new status is defined, is at least in part written by the participant.

The taking of a magical name within Wicca is one way the participant helps to create her or his own transformation. Participants normally choose their own magical names and determine when they need new ones. Arachne warned a group of neophytes that they should be very careful when they choose a magical name, as the name provides a framework for their personal growth. She advised that if they select the name of a goddess or god they should fully research all aspects of that deity. The high priest of the same coven told me later that when one is going through a major life change it is helpful to develop a new magical name, one that will provide a focus for that change. Three Blade Jaguar's naming ceremony is a good example of this process. He decided to take a new name when his life circumstances changed. During his naming ritual he told us that he had adopted his name because it acknowledged him as a guardian and guide to his son and as a protector of his family and his people. The name was chosen by him and his high priestess from their readings of Mexican mythology.

Unlike in traditional societies, in which rites of passage are socially determined, Three Blade Jaguar chose the time for the ritual to change his name and identity. The name he chose—and the names that most Wiccans adopt—are directly or in style taken from other cultures. The names become separated from their cultural context. Giddens contends that late modernity distinguishes itself from traditional societies because social institutions become "disembedded," separated from a situated place and lived time. Clearly, this is the case with magical names, which have lost whatever meaning they may have had within the symbolic system of the culture from which they are derived. The name becomes reinterpreted within a new context. Because the names derive from a variety of cultures, the meaning of the name is not universally understood, even within the Neo-Pagan community. Three Blade Jaguar told us the meaning of his old and new names during the ritual. He will repeat this process at Neo-Pagan gatherings where he will inform people of his new magical name and its significance.

In defining his name, Three Blade Jaguar suggested that it indicated that he was the protector of his people, a phrase spoken at every rite of passage for a male Witch that I have attended. The phrase is a romantic fiction since there is no longer a single tribe to which everyone belongs. In part this is an attempt to rhetorically create a link to traditional societies; it is also an indication of the difficulty in late modernity of defining the gendered self. What does it mean to be a man in the late twentieth century, particularly for men within a religion with a strong feminist component? The construction of self, particularly a gendered self, is something that is being negotiated. While the phrase "protector of his people" is empty, it implies a positive image of traditional manhood.

THE GENDERED SELF

The self as it is developed within Wiccan rituals is a gendered self. Some rituals, particularly those that surround puberty or menopause, speak directly to issues of gender, while in others gender is more subtly displayed. McGuire (1994) argues that in the last thirty years, due to the development of a more fluid definition of maleness and femaleness, all religions must confront the issue of gender either by reinforcing traditional gender roles or suggesting new ones. As Witchcraft is self-consciously a feminist form of spirituality, gender roles are both questioned and played with.

Participants in Wicca are disproportionally female. In the Neo-Pagan census we found that women composed 65 percent of the respondents and 15.9 percent were men; 19.1 percent did not respond to this question

(H. Berger et al. n.d.). In Orion's survey, in which she received only 189 responses, 38 percent of respondents were male, 58 percent were female, and 4 percent claimed to be androgynous (Orion 1995:62). The unwillingness to identify one's gender, or to accept the category as dichotomous, is a reflection of gender politics. For at least some Witches, the issue is irrelevant or requires a new definition. Nonetheless, we can estimate that 65–75 percent of all participants are women; 25–35 percent men. My subjective sense of the New England Neo-Pagan community has been that men compose about 40 percent of the community. This may in part be because I have focused on groups that include both men and women. There are many more all-women's groups than all-men's groups, which would skew the survey data. The strong feminist component and the emphasis on goddess worship draw many more women than men to this form of religion.

Robbins and Bromley argue that new religious movements are "laboratories of social experimentation . . . [that] often contribute to a subterranean cultural tradition constituting a cultural resource pool for mobilizing protest and experimenting with new patterns and styles" (1992:1). Witchcraft is mentioned by Robbins and Bromley as one of these "social laboratories" that they view as offering a cultural resource for alternative gender roles for women. They note that through identification with the goddess(es) women are encouraged to transcend traditional gender roles of passivity and dependence.

WOMEN'S GENDER ROLES

Wiccan rituals are designed to increase women's sense of power and to help them recognize their own will. As Witchcraft is an anti-authoritarian religion that celebrates the lack of a central authority that determines orthodoxy, there is no one set of belief or practices about appropriate gender roles within this religion. However, certain trends can be discerned.

A number of scholars have described rituals that are oriented toward the redefinition of women's gender roles and re-empowerment of the participants (Neitz 1991; Griffin 1995; Jacobs 1991, 1989; McGuire 1988). Griffin, who studied two all-women's Witchcraft groups, chronicles three rituals she attended in which there was a redefinition of the three aspects of woman: the maid, the mother, and the crone. According to Griffin, each of these rituals provided the participants with alternative images of womanhood to the virgin madonna, who is defined by her role as mother. In the ritual for the maid, Diana, the goddess of the hunt, was portrayed by a large woman, whose form would have been intimidating to many in mundane life and was made more powerful within the ritual. This is no chaste virgin who fears going out in the world; this is an independent woman, who during the ritual appears coming across a moonlit field, bare-breasted. She is the goddess, an element of all women, young, strong, capable, and independent. The image of Mary, the mother, was transformed from the mother of God to the goddess of fertility who has a material body, is sexual, and produces life from her body. The ritual for the crone also challenged the traditional image of the old woman as withered and spent and offered instead a vision of old age as a time of power. Griffin reports that women who attended each of these rituals related that they felt they were offered new possibilities for defining themselves as women.

Eller (1993), examining women's-only Witchcraft groups, describes the use of both rituals and alternative medical practices as means for women to heal themselves from the maltreatment they have suffered in a male-dominated society. The metaphor of healing is used by Eller to describe the transformation of the self:[9] "In spiritual feminist thought, it is a given that all women need healing: if not from specific illnesses or infirmities, then from the pains suffered as a result of growing up female in a patriarchal world. Spiritual feminists aspire to healing themselves and their sisters through a variety of less than medically and psychotherapeutically orthodox techniques" (109).

Although these authors focus on exclusively women's groups, I have attended similar rituals for women in inclusive groups. The croning ritual for Renenutet, the high priestess of MoonTide coven, involved fewer people than the one described by Griffin, but it also emphasized the crone as powerful, desirable, and sexually active, as well as wise.

Renenutet's croning ritual was attended by both women and men; other women's rituals of inclusive groups that I have attended have been unisex. At one Neo-Pagan gathering a women's-only ritual was called in the late morning. The festival was attended by approximately six hundred women, men, and children; of that about sixty women participated in the ritual. Other rituals and classes were taking place at the same time; these occupied some of the people who did not attend the women's circle. As always at festivals, some people used the time to sleep, write, meditate, do their work assignment, or visit with others around the ritual fire or on the grass.

The women's ritual lasted several hours. Each element of the ritual was aimed at having the women, like snakes, shed their old skins and develop new ones. The women assembled at a clearing at the edge of the

this new religion by his brother: "I'll never forget his opening line was, 90 percent of all murders in the world are committed by men—65 percent of the victims are women and children; 99 percent of all homicides including war, etc., are committed by men; 55–60 percent of the victims are women and children. He spent five hours talking about goddess and the evils of patriarchy and so forth; by the time he was done I had a case of the born agains" (David Mayfire Interview 1995). David Mayfire believes, as many Witches and Neo-Pagans do, that he was not so much converted to Neo-Paganism as that he found a term that describes the way he and his wife have always lived—loving and venerating nature. Even though he keeps his religious affiliation secret from his fundamentalist neighbors and clients, he has decorated his home as well as his office with pictures of the goddess. She is for him an important image of his connection to nature and to the divine.

Although men's and women's responses to the image of the goddess have similarities, there are significant differences. Women who worship the goddess see her as affirming themselves and their bodies. Women's menstruation, ability to give birth, and menopause are all acknowledged through the veneration of the goddess. Women's bodies are not viewed as sinful, but as sites of joy, magic, and in some cases holiness. Men's bodies and reproductive functions are clearly not reflected in the image of the goddess; however, men who worship the goddess do identify with her—they see the goddess as a representation of their female "selves" or female energy.

Although there is a good deal of variance among groups, a widespread notion within Wicca is that all people have male and female aspects, or energies, which can be nurtured and developed. The veneration of the goddess is viewed as one way men can come in contact with their feminine selves. The goddess provides these men with models of powerful female behavior, affect, and attitudes. Men also join workshops, which are held at festivals, occult shops, and at times within covens, to commune with their female energies. According to my male informants, these workshops can take several forms. Groups may participate in the equivalent of a lay therapy session, in which men talk about their attempts, failures, and successes in working with their female energy. In some workshops, particular goddesses and their forms of energy are explored, while in others rituals are developed to help men get in touch with the goddess or a particular goddess.

Within Wicca the concept of female energies or selves is loosely interpreted. Janet and Stewart Farrar (1992:111) provide the clearest definition: "The strength of the female nature is intuitive and cyclical, emphasizing a situation's totality." On the other hand, male nature "is intellectual and linear emphasizing a situation's statistics" (Farrar and Farrar 1992:111). According to the Farrars, both men and women possess elements of male and female natures. Although the Farrars' definition of gender roles is more conservative than that of many Witches, an element of their definition permeates goddess worship. The feminine is regularly associated with nurturing, caring, and communality. Even concepts of the goddess as the bearer of death focus on death as part of the process of renewal, not as annihilation. Through developing their feminine side, male Witches separate themselves from patriarchal forms of domination of nature and of women. They are also attempting to obliterate those aspects of male socialization that they see as interfering with the formation of a "saner" world. Men, through coming in touch with their feminine sides, are hoping to develop a healthier psyche, one that is more open to their own feelings and to connections with other people.

All the groups that are inclusive of men and women worship the god as well as the goddess. Within Wiccan mythology the god is viewed as transforming from the goddess's son to her consort. While the goddess is eternal, the god is born, matures, and then dies, only to be reborn. As with the goddess, some Wiccans view all the gods as manifestations of one god; others see each of the gods as distinct. David Mayfire, in speaking of the gods, contended, "Even though in Neo-Paganism we have been hiding from a lot of male energy because of patriarchy, these gods at least at one time must have had a more positive form—definitely there is such a thing as male energy. Male aggression is natural; it doesn't have to be put to evil purposes" (David Mayfire Interview 1995).

Identification with the god is equivalent to identification with the goddess, except that it places one in touch with one's male self or energy. Women may feel the need to come in touch with their male energy and may invoke the gods, or a particular god. However, it is much more common for men to attempt to develop female selves. As David Mayfire notes, there is ambivalence about "male energy," which is often associated with patriarchy in the Neo-Pagan community. But many Neo-Pagan men turn to the gods for a positive image of maleness. In *Earth God Rising: The Return of the Male Mysteries* (1990:xii) Alan Richardson notes, "Those world problems caused by the negative aspects of the male dominated societies can be cured not solely by reaching toward the female aspects of divinity, but by invoking those forgotten and positive aspects of our most ancient god. The Horned God is just, never cruel; firm but never vindictive. The Horned God loves women as equals."

For many male Witches, the gods provide a positive image of manhood, which they view as distinct from the patriarchal conception of being a man. Through coming in touch with and developing their links to the goddess and through the emulation of the old gods, male Witches are attempting to develop a nonsexist, positive image of manhood in the late twentieth century.

As are women, men are encouraged to question traditional gender role behavior. I have seen heterosexual as well as homosexual men wearing skirts at festivals and sabbat celebrations. The larger community encourages men to break through traditional gender roles, to get in touch with their feelings, to become involved with their children, and to do work that is traditionally within the women's sphere. Ceisiwr Serith (1991:7), writing about his experience at a men's gathering, noted, "These men, who had spoken from the heart and bared their wounds in council all weekend were nonetheless hard. They were strong. They were powerful. They were proud. There is no need to be either a Sensitive New Age Guy or a John Wayne. We had found a third way." The third way, however, remains somewhat shadowy. Positive images of manhood are less clearly defined than positive female images. Women are encouraged to become empowered, to gain control over their lives, and to question patriarchal attitudes. Men, too, are asked to question patriarchal attitudes, to become more caring and nurturing. Nonetheless, the images for a man are those of the protector or guardian of his people. This image is less clearly translated into daily life activities than the images provided for women.

Homosexuality and Polarity

In "The Pagan Census" we found that 68 percent of the respondents were heterosexual; 4.8 percent were lesbians; 4.6 percent gay men; 18.7 percent were bisexual; 4 percent claimed to be "other." Homosexual and bisexual women and men are drawn to the religion, at least in part, because of its open acceptance of them and their sexuality. Some groups, usually those that define themselves as Dianics, are composed completely of lesbians and bisexual women, while others are composed of gay men. All the inclusive groups that I have met have been open to individuals regardless of sexual orientation. The large presence of gays and lesbians, as well as the commitment to diversity, alternative lifestyles, and openness, has resulted in the questioning of some of the traditional ritual practices within Wicca.

The rituals as Gardner originally presented them and as they continue to be practiced incorporate the polarity between male and female elements. It is common within rituals, particularly fertility rituals, for the men and women to form two different groups to enact this polarity. Furthermore, some of the imagery—such as the atheme, or ritual knife, being equated with the male and the cup with the female—implies a gender specificity. The direct or implied heterosexual implications have been challenged particularly by lesbians and gay men, who feel their own sexuality is being diminished by being viewed as "less fertile." A twenty-eight-year-old lesbian noted,

> Gender and polarity are not the same thing. Protons, (neutrons), and electrons do not have sexes as we understand them.
> . . . Gay men and lesbians have, in general, the ability and equipment for reproduction and we do reproduce actually, so I don't see why it is so difficult for many Pagans (gay and straight) to understand why we can participate in fertility rites with no hassles. . . . (Why should a goddess force only be invoked on a priestess, for example? This is silly). (H. Berger and A. Arthen n.d.:1425)

Because of this challenge from within the community, changes in ritual practice and language have occurred, along with resistance to those changes. The Circle of Light coven changed its Beltane ritual after it had initiated several gay and lesbian members. The ritual as it initially was performed required that the women enter the temple first and consecrate it. When they were ready, the women sent a representative to call the men to enter the temple. The polarity of male and female was carried throughout the ritual. One of the initiates to the coven, a lesbian, was quite vocal about her feeling that this ritual did not fully include her and her sexuality. Although initially there was resistance to change in this coven's last Beltane celebration that I attended, the polarity was changed to seed bearers and earth keepers. People were asked to choose their own role. All the men chose to be seed bearers, as did three of the women.

Similarly, at an open Beltane ritual for EarthSpirit, participants were asked to choose between digging the hole for the maypole to be placed in, and going into the woods to find the pole—depending on the "energy" each person was presently working with. Some men chose to stay and help dig the hole, although the group going into the woods had more of a balance of men and women than those staying behind. In earlier EarthSpirit maypole rituals that I attended (at both their open rituals in the Boston area and the ritual at their large spring festival in western Massachusetts,

Rites of Spring), the division had been made along gender lines. There had been an open debate about changing this division in the EarthSpirit newsletter. Those who opposed the change had cited tradition; those who prevailed called for the reevaluation of gender roles and inclusion of gay and lesbian participants.

THE NEW WOMAN? THE NEW MAN?

Palmer (1994), based on a review of Allen's (1987), Aidala's (1985), and Reuther's (1983) work as well as her own research, has developed a typology of gender identity within new religious movements. She suggests that religions tend to view the sexes in one of three ways: one, women and men are regarded as spiritually polar opposites who have only stylized interactions with one another; two, the sexes are perceived as complementary, each requiring the other to become complete or whole spiritually; three, men and women are viewed as essentially alike. Witchcraft does not fit neatly into this typology. All-women's groups differ in defining women's gender roles as separate from men's. In groups that include both men and women, there appears to be a tension between the view of masculine and feminine, if not the sexes themselves, as complementary and the view of men and women as essentially the same. Joe, a Neo-Pagan, sums up this ambivalence:

> Women tend to be more talented in intuitive areas—men more prone to physical areas—things mechanical—I think there are some things that women are naturally better at and vice versa. Let's put is this way—women are probably better at magic than men. In fact I am almost sure that women are better at magic than men. I think men make better warriors—I think men just adapt to that better—it may be societal upbringing, I don't know. The gap is very narrow—the difference in their abilities is negligible enough that it shouldn't stop them from doing it. Our priestess fights and I do magic. (Joe Interview 1987)

Joe's vacillation about the existence and extent of differences between the sexes—let alone whether these differences are innate or a result of socialization—is reflected not only in the Wiccan community but within feminist literature as well (Pollitt 1992). Elements of essentialism—the belief that men and women are innately different in their responses and abilities—coexist with attempts to create a community of equity between men and women within Wicca.

The efforts to create gender equality do not, however, mean that sexism has been obliterated. A forty-six-year-old heterosexual woman asserted: "I think half the men who get involved in Pagan/Wicca stuff do it as a ploy to get laid. And the other half are trying to prove that they're better 'Witches' than women. Poor babies" (H. Berger and A. Arthen n.d.:1307). The open sexuality and nudity at Neo-Pagan gatherings offer the opportunity for some men to act in a sexually aggressive manner. At one festival that I attended, a group of women confronted Larry, who was accused of sexually harassing several women. It is common at gatherings for people to hug and kiss hello. Larry, however, went past the accepted level of affection, to touching and tongue-kissing women, who objected to his behavior. After rebuking Larry, the women spoke to the organizers of the festival and demanded that Larry be removed from the premises if there was another incident. His behavior was not tolerated by either the women, the organizer, or the general community.

On the one hand, the women were supported in controlling negative male behavior. On the other hand, even though Larry was a Neo-Pagan, a participant in feminist spirituality, he was also acting in a sexually aggressive fashion. It is unclear how involved Larry was in the religion. The amorphous nature of Neo-Paganism means that, possibly more than in other religions and groups, people attend festivals who are only marginally involved. Although I do not think that Larry is typical of Neo-Pagan men, his behavior is not unique. Pike (1996:134–36) similarly describes the occurrence of sexual harassment at festivals. This behavior is one indication of the difficulty of changing traditional gender roles, even in a group committed to equality.

The worship of the goddess provides one response to the second wave of feminism. Unlike some fundamentalist religions that reject the feminist's claims out of hand, Wicca incorporates feminism. Issues of gender are central to this new religion. However, even with this commitment there continue to be elements of the traditional notion of manhood and womanhood. Women and men who worship the goddess as well as the gods are attempting to create new images of manhood and womanhood, based both on modern interpretations of a mythical past and on the demands of feminism. They have not produced the "new person," but they are part of a process of questioning gender roles. Rituals, magic, and mysticism are all involved in the process of self-creation. Part of this process is the attempt to create new behavior patterns for both men and women.

CHAPTER 3

The Coven

Perfect Love, Perfect Trust

On Saturday, March 21, 1987, at its first sabbat, the Circle of Light coven was officially established. The ten members of the group, six women and four men, gathered for the festival in Arachne and Gabriel's small basement apartment. The spring equinox had been chosen as an auspicious time for the official opening of the coven. As Gabriel contended, "In spring, trees and plants are budding and flowering; the flow of nature is in tune for growth and change."

There was a rush of excitement in the group as members moved living room furniture and neatly stacked it in the hall of the apartment building. The living room was transformed into an open carpeted space that quickly became a temple. Altars were formed on each of the four walls, using tables covered in brightly colored silken cloth. The color of the cloth corresponded to the direction of the altar—yellow for east, red for south, aqua for west, and black for north. On each altar were a vase of freshly cut flowers, candles in the appropriate color, and symbols of that direction. It took less than half an hour to visually transform the secular living space of two graduate students to a sacred space prepared for ritual.

Arachne and Gabriel's bedroom served as a changing room. As people finished carrying furniture or setting up altars they moved into the bedroom, threw off their blue jeans, shirts, sweaters, and underwear, and put on their newly made blue ritual robes. Elbows and knees collided as people jammed into the small bedroom to change. Some people waited to enter the crowded room until the first wave of participants had moved out. Clothing was strewn over the double bed, floor, and dresser in overlapping piles. The small neat bedroom took on the appearance of a stereotypical teenager's abode, with clothing peeking out from all corners. The four "elders," those who had been in the craft longest and had reached second degree, belted their robes with red braided rope. Everyone else wore white ropes as belts. Ritual jewelry, such as crystals, goddess symbols, and pentagrams, was worn by both men and women.

An almost electric energy could be felt in the living room, as people milled around waiting for the ritual to begin. Everyone was in high spirits—joking, laughing, and telling stories. After checking that all the altars were correctly arranged and that matches were available to light the candles and incense, Arachne asked that we sit in a circle and prepare ourselves psychologically for the ritual. The lights were dimmed and everyone sat quietly, concentrating on centering—that is, eliminating from one's mind the mundane thoughts and concerns of the day and becoming open for the ritual. To help everyone focus and calm down, Arachne led the group in a breathing exercise. We all were told to bring in air in long breaths and then to let them go. The room was now quiet, filled only with the sounds of people breathing. One person started making an OM sound and all followed. The sound echoed around the sparsely furnished room, filling it and refilling it as the sound increased and decreased in strength for several minutes. When silence descended on the room, Arachne requested that we stand to add our energy to the casting of the circle, which was done by her and Gabriel. Each of the quarters was called by a different participant.

Although most subsequent sabbats were open to outside guests, this one was closed to all but group members. The ritual, which was written by the elders, had the focus of all spring equinox rituals—the coming of the spring, the time of renewal. As part of one poem in the ritual noted,

> Spring has come up from the south again,
> With soft winds in her hair,
> And a warm wind in her mouth again
> And budding everywhere.[1]

This ritual was unique, however, because it ended with each of the participants going through a long V-shaped human tunnel formed by the coven members, standing one behind the other and spreading their legs. This, we were told by Arachne, was the birth canal, through which we would each pass to be reborn within the coven. The last person on the line, Beth, lay down on her back, and the people above her helped her move through the human tunnel. As she emerged at the other end, Gabriel rang a bell and announced her magical name. Beth now became the first in the line. The next person made his way through the tunnel until everyone, including Gabriel, had passed through. The process of moving on one's back through this tunnel of legs was difficult. Laughter rippled and resounded in the living room, as people made fun of their own awkwardness, the attempts of the people above to help them, and the peeks of flesh as people crawled between one another's legs and as robes shifted during movement through the tunnel. The ritual was fun, but it was also a serious process of creating a group spirit and an avenue for commitment.

The feast, a potluck dinner that follows all rituals, was more elaborate than usual. Within Witchcraft circles, the ability to cook, sew, or make handcrafted articles is highly prized and encouraged, as part of the ideology of returning to a simpler time, when people's lives were more in synchrony with nature and community life. The dinners after rituals usually involve culinary delights. This evening's feast included freshly baked bread, roast turkey, pasta salad, and an array of homemade desserts. During the feast Beth remarked on how difficult it was to get through the coven's "birth canal." Arachne proposed that the struggle was reminiscent of an infant's entry into the world through its mother's birth canal: "One must struggle to be born, into the world and into the coven."

The Circle of Light coven had been meeting for six weeks determining the direction the group would take and developing camaraderie. One potential member, an African-American woman, the only person of color in the group, decided not to join because of the pressing demands of her work, graduate courses, and singing practice. The original group going through the human tunnel was composed of four men and six women, including me. Arachne, Gabriel, Gail, and Steve were the elders. Gail, then in her thirties, was the oldest member of the group; the other three elders were in their twenties, the same age as the other participants. Arachne and Gabriel are married. Gail, who often referred to Arachne as her coven sister, had received her first and second degree at the same time and in the same coven as Arachne. Steve had been trained by a group in a nearby state. After meeting the other three elders through Neo-Pagan circles, he had been invited to participate in the new coven's formation.

As mentioned in the preface, I had been invited to join as a researcher after meeting three of the elders at my public talk on witchcraft at the Boston Public Library. Linda and Oscar, who had recently come to Boston from the Midwest, met Arachne at another public talk that I gave at Boston University. After I finished speaking, Linda asked if I could introduce her to Witches in the Boston vicinity as she and her husband had only recently moved to the area. Arachne interceded, inviting Linda and her husband to come to the next meeting of the group. The other members—Carol, a short, blond, and engaging biologist in her twenties; Barry, a computer analyst, in his twenties, short, heavyset with a full beard; and Beth, in her early twenties, attractive and attempting to complete a degree in biology—were found either through Neo-Pagan circles or through an advertisement the elders placed in occult bookstores and Neo-Pagan journals. Most of the people entered the group as strangers and through the next months became friends. The metaphor used repeatedly to express the import of these relationships was *the coven is like a family*.[2]

SOLO VERSUS GROUP PRACTITIONERS

Not all Witches belong to a coven; some individuals practice alone or with a romantic partner. "The Pagan Census" found that 50.4 percent of the respondents were at the time of the survey solo practitioners (H. Berger et al. n.d.). One respondent explained why she is no longer in a group: "I have participated in group rituals, but found that the personal conflict and turmoil interfered with spiritual and magical growth. Therefore I am solo once again" (H. Berger and A. Arthen n.d.:2503). Most Witches are solo practitioners for some period of time. The reasons for solo practice vary: some individuals prefer to work alone and never join a coven; others, like the respondent quoted, leave groups due to conflicts or the disbandment of the coven; still others are solo practitioners at the beginning of their career as Witches, prior to joining a coven.

Most members of Wicca are converts, having joined the religion in their twenties. As with other new religions, some people join, stay for a while, and then move on to another religion or secularism. Becoming a Witch, however, is somewhat different from joining other new religions: one can join the religion without ever coming in direct contact with another practitioner. One can simply read a book or journal and declare oneself a Witch.

Daniel, eighteen years old and in his first year of college, declared himself a Witch when he was in high school. He had been raised as a Catholic, but became alienated from the church both because of its hierarchical structure and his sense of exclusion as a gay male. Like many Witches, he believes that he has always been inclined to the craft, even before he knew that it had a name. He became a Witch after reading several books on Wicca, which he found at an occult bookstore. Through his readings and his own intuition, he has developed rituals for sabbats and esabats. He said that he might want to work with a group, but had not met other Witches with whom he felt he could work and learn.

Daniel's isolation is greater than many solitary practitioners that I know. Tammy, for instance, a woman in her thirties who defines herself as a solo practitioner, sometimes does magical workings with other Witches and joins open circles for the sabbats. She feels that some magical workings require the energy of more people and enjoys the social aspects of joining with others for holidays. Daniel's youth may contribute to his isolation. He defines himself as a novice who has not had the opportunity to meet other people through festivals and gatherings. Daniel may remain on the periphery of Witchcraft, reading some books and journals and never becoming integrated into the community. However, since he has been open about his religious beliefs and practices in several of his classes, he will probably meet other people at his college who are also Witches. A small but active group on his campus is talking about forming an official club. Through the networks of Witchcraft organizations, in universities, and in the larger world, novices usually learn about groups they can join, computer networks they can browse, and the availability of publications.

Both Tammy and Daniel have chosen to work as solitaries, neither of them having joined a coven. However, most Wiccans who stay in the religion do join a coven at some point in their career. Coven training is viewed by many in the Neo-Pagan community as necessary to becoming a *real* Witch. In the Neo-Pagan census a thirty-year-old woman complained, "I am mostly self-taught, with books, seminars, and informal training from others. I have met derision and outright scorn from other members of the Wiccan/Pagan community" (H. Berger and A. Arthen n.d.:1342). Although no formal criteria exist for someone to become a Witch, those in integrated groups hold that coven membership is important for a person to be fully trained. This is true, even though as mentioned in chapter 1, membership in individual covens is fluid.

When the Circle of Light coven dissolved in the fall of 1996, only Arachne and Gabriel were still fully participating. Steve and Carol, who met in the coven, are married and have a child. They dropped out of the Circle of Light coven and practiced on their own for three years, returning to participate in events at the Circle of Light several years ago. The other original members of the coven have dispersed. Linda and Oscar have started their own coven. Beth has moved out of the state, although she did attend rituals with the Circle of Light when she was in town. New people joined the coven, and many of the old faces reappeared at sabbats or at other Neo-Pagan gatherings.

Arachne and Gabriel became tired of running the coven, organizing sabbats, and repeatedly training a new group of neophytes. They unsuccessfully attempted to turn over leadership of the coven to another couple. If the coven had been passed to new leaders it would have continued, albeit with none of the original members. Instead, at the 1996 fall equinox—the period of death in nature—the Circle of Light coven closed. Unlike its beginning, the coven's end was not accompanied by a special ceremony. At its last official sabbat no vows of recommitment to the coven were given. Some Wiccans view the fall equinox as a time to either renew or permit to die vows and commitments of the previous year. The Circle of Light, born on the spring equinox in 1987, completed its life cycle and died almost a decade later on the fall equinox.

The instability of covens and other Neo-Pagan groups has lead Neitz (1994) to call Wicca a quasi-religion, whose social import rests in its being a source of cultural change. Although this perspective has value, I think it is limited in that it does not examine the role of social networks beyond their ability to transmit alternative cultural metaphors and symbols. But covens are, among other things, friendship groups, whose role in the formation of networks and interlocking associations is important to understanding the functioning of Wicca.

"The coven is a place of perfect love and perfect trust," Arachne stated several times as the Circle of Light coven was being formed.[3] This is the ideal of the coven—a place of safety and care as well as a place to join with others in ritual and magical practices. The eventual disintegration of most covens and the transience of their membership might appear to belie the notion of the coven as a place of perfect love and perfect trust. However, as in modern marriages and families, the transience of personal relationships does not mean those ties are unimportant, either in immediate or long-term relationships.

FRIENDSHIP

Both friendship and kin relationships have been transformed in modernity. The growth in abstract systems—such as bureaucracies, commodified markets, urbanization, and expert knowledge—has resulted in the disembedding of the individual from a specific time and space as well as from an array of personal relationships. In traditional societies most interactions were based on personal relationships, whether they were with friends, family members, or local healers. Friendships in premodern societies were predicated on a notion of insiders versus outsiders; those who were neither kin nor friends were enemies. Friendships were institutionalized based on mutual defense and aid. In modernity, on the other hand, the stranger is not necessarily an enemy, but might be an acquaintance, a colleague, or someone we pass on the street (Giddens 1990:118).

Friendships are relationships of choice. Although many friendships are formed at work or in neighborhoods, others are increasingly chosen because of shared interests (Fischer 1982). These are "pure relationships" in that they are separated from the immediate contingencies of economic need or power relations. According to Giddens, pure relationships have seven components:

1. These relationships are "free-floating"—separated from the necessities of social or economic life.
2. The relationships are fragile because they are completely based on the desire to be together.
3. The relationships are based on reflexivity, as participants examine whether the relationship is working or not.
4. Pure relationships are sustained by commitment, which has replaced the older anchors of economic and political necessity.
5. Central to pure relationships is a quest for intimacy, which is based in part on a shared and meaningful lifestyle. Intimacy requires work, as people strive to open themselves up to one another.
6. For individuals to feel safe in their attempts to establish intimacy, there must be trust within these relationships.
7. Through these relationships individuals find their self-identity affirmed. (Giddens 1991:94–97)

Giddens's typology must be viewed as an ideal type. Clearly, even in modernity intimate relationships have economic and political components, as is witnessed by the growth of books on networking for career or financial success. As Rubin in an early work on friendship (1985) notes, there is a distinction between the ideals of friendship and the actual experience of being friends. The ideals of friendship that she found in her research correspond to those mentioned by Giddens: "trust, honesty, respect, commitment, safety, support, generosity, loyalty, mutuality, constancy, understanding, acceptance" (Rubin 1985:7). However, the reality is more complex, as individuals do not always conform to the ideal. Furthermore, Giddens does not adequately distinguish between friendship and kinship. Although both have been transformed in modernity, friendship and erotic relationships more clearly than kinship have been radically separated from the claims of obligation that still linger in family relationships. As the respondents in Rubin's studies suggested, friends, unlike family members, are chosen. The ability to choose friends is central in understanding their importance in the development of self-identity and the development of life politics (Friedman 1995; Fischer 1982; Rubin 1985; Giddens 1990, 1991).

Individuals choose friends who will help them develop aspects of their personality or who share the same commitments as themselves. Although there has been movement toward pure relationships ever since the development of an urban industrial society, this has become more dramatic in late modernity. Even more important than the actual growth of dense urban populations is the ability of large numbers of people to communicate over time and space, which has increased with the availability of computers, Internet links, and fax machines (Webber 1970). Increasingly, individuals can pick their friends from a wide geographic area, which permits them to find people who most support their lifestyle and political commitments.

Although friends take on particular importance in the development of self-identity in the context of late modernity, the actuality or at least the symbolism of family remains integral. Rubin's study suggests that families remain for most people the place of last resort. Rubin quotes from Robert Frost: "Home is the place where, when you have to go there, / They have to take you in" (1985:22). The notion of the family as less supportive of life choices is juxtaposed with the notion of the family's remaining a less voluntary institution than friendship and hence a safer one. The family as a metaphor for intimacy remains important within friendship groups. Close friends, like coven mates, are frequently described as like family. The desire to be like a family is in part a response to the fragility of friendship relationships, which can as easily be terminated as begun.

BECOMING FRIENDS IN THE COVEN

According to Starhawk, "The coven is a Witches' support group, consciousness-raising group, psychic study center, clergy-training program, College of Mysteries, surrogate clan, and religious congregation all rolled into one" (1979:35). The coven in some ways resembles a congregation. The members regularly join together for a series of activities, some of which are more clearly oriented toward worship than others. There is a round of visiting, sharing of work, and development of a variety of loosely defined activities (Lofland and Richardson 1984). Covens are local groups and have no full-time employees to organize or run them. Covens, like congregations, participate in "worship, education, mission, stewardship . . . [and] what may be the master function of congregations in such a pluralistic society as the United States: fellowship" (Warner 1994:64). Unlike the congregation, however, the coven does not have a separate building that is its *centerpiece*. The lack of a center, separate from any of the members' homes, is part of the reason that covens so easily disintegrate. As people drift away from the coven, move to another state, or break away in anger, there is no ongoing bureaucracy, as would be necessitated by owning a building. Nor is there the building itself to remain the focus of activity.

The coven is, in Greil and Rudy's terms (1984), a social cocoon that encapsulates the individuals to encourage the process of socialization into new behaviors, social roles, values, and conceptions of self. As Witches remain active in the larger world—working, going to school, visiting with non-Wiccan family and friends—they are not, as in some new religious movements, cut off from the larger community. However, the coven becomes the focus of people's lives because of the large time commitment required by the coven and the growth of intimacy among those who belong. The coven trains individuals in ritual and magical practices and also socializes them into a world of mysticism, ecological concerns, and feminism. The closeness of the group helps to foster changes in individuals' lives and perspectives. This is not to suggest that people become brainwashed or are psychologically disabled from leaving the coven. The rate at which covens dissolve and individuals break from a group is a clear refutation of any notion that people are caught in a group they cannot leave. Those who join a Wiccan coven do so because they have already embraced a magical worldview. This view is further developed and refined in the cocoon of the coven.

The Circle of Light coven defined itself as a training coven—that is, one in which neophytes are taught ritual practice and magic. Initially the direction of the coven was unclear. Steve, one of the elders, confided that he was originally surprised and discomforted by many of the members' lack of experience in Wicca. He had hoped to find a group of equals in which to work magic and participate in rituals. However, it soon became clear that many of the people who were participating were neophytes who came with only a smattering of knowledge gleaned from books, journals, and attendance at some festivals. Arachne and Gabriel had from the onset been pleased with the idea of creating a teaching coven, one in which the neophytes would be trained and eventually "hive-off to create their own covens." They would be creating a network of groups, all of which could trace their origins back to the Circle of Light coven.

Through the classes and meetings that were required to train people and also provide a structure to the coven, the participants moved from strangers to intimates. The group met at least once a week for classes or meetings, as well as every two weeks for esabats and every six weeks for sabbats. During the first year I missed a few of the classes due to scheduling problems. As I did not become an initiate, I was excluded from some of the classes in the second year that dealt with finer points of magic and magical practice.

The early meetings were usually held at Arachne and Gabriel's home, which was centrally located. As the group evolved, there was some attempt to rotate the location of the meetings and rituals. The original purpose of this rotation was to relieve Arachne and Gabriel of hosting all the events; however, a secondary effect, as Gail noted, was "We will get to know one another better if we visit each other's homes." Nonetheless, most of the meetings and rituals continued to be held at Arachne and Gabriel's home, as they more and more clearly became the high priestess and priest. When they moved from their small basement apartment to a larger sunny apartment on the second floor of a private home, the second bedroom was converted into a temple. The creation of a permanent temple helped to cement their home as the covenstead, where people met for rituals, classes, and "to just hang out." When the third-floor apartment in the same private home became available, Linda and Oscar moved in, making the house even more clearly the center of group activity.

That the coven worked to create intimacy was apparent—more so than with other friendships—as it was structured into the group process. Each group meeting began with a "check-in" session, in which everyone spoke for a few minutes about how their week had gone and how they were feeling. In the early weeks of the group, people talked mostly about their concerns with work, more frequently focusing on problems but at times also reporting successes they were experiencing. Those members still in school spoke about their course work or the process of completing their doctoral research. Although throughout my fieldnotes I recorded that people always returned to issues centering on school and work, there was also an increased sharing of information about people's personal lives— fears, pleasures, and problems in their love lives, with parents, or with other friends. A sense of trust grew and with it came a growing amount of intimacy.

As this was a coven and not merely a social group, individuals were encouraged to share spiritual experiences. Oscar, at the beginning of one meeting, told us of his encounter with the goddess. He had been home alone one evening watching logs burn in his fireplace. As he meditated, the goddess came to him and brought him through the veil that separates the living and the dead. He came to the world of the spirit and realized how peaceful and joyous it is. He felt himself transformed as his fear of death and dying evaporated. He was now better able to sleep at night, as he no longer feared the coming of death.

My fieldnotes mention my initial discomfort at the process of checking in, which I had uncomplimentarily labeled *pop-psych*. But as the weeks went by, it became evident that, although the weekly sharing was routinized, it was effective in creating intimacy. It also served as a process of training people in interactive skills. At the third meeting of the group, Arachne stated that, based on Starhawk's writings, we would have a facilitator for the meeting. According to Starhawk, the facilitator's role is to ensure that people stay on the topic, speak in turn, and do not interrupt one another (Starhawk 1982:116). For Starhawk, as well as for the members of the Circle of Light coven, the use of the facilitator helps ensure that the group process does not result in a few people's dominating the conversation and therefore the decision-making process. It is an attempt to move away from hierarchial forms of power to power sharing.

In my fieldnotes I wrote, "The facilitator is encouraging everyone to participate in what Lakoff referred to as women's ways of speaking." Lakoff (1976) notes that men are more likely than women to change the topic of conversation, to interrupt, and to negatively comment on what the other person has said.[4] On the other hand, women, according to Lakoff, are more likely to give cues for others to continue speaking, help to maintain the present discussion, and give support for the other person's position even when they disagree. Part of the facilitator's job, therefore, is to retrain people into an interactive pattern that will decrease the development of *power over* and facilitate *power to*. Although the rules of discourse are applied universally, they are rules that grew out of feminist research and thought.

Before the initiation of the coven, the weekly meetings focused on issues surrounding the structure of the coven and expectations of the members. For example, at one meeting to pick a name for the coven, several names were suggested and discussed until a consensus was reached. At another meeting we spoke about making matching ritual robes. As colors are magically charged, each associated with a direction and a particular set of powers, the decision about the robes' hue had as much, if not more, to do with the developing conception of the coven's purpose as with aesthetics. After a lengthy discussion about the virtue of several colors, the group decided on either purple or blue. Although there seemed to be more support for purple than blue when the group met that Saturday to buy the fabric, we purchased a dutch blue cotton and polyester blend. This material was chosen because it was inexpensive, enough yardage was available to make ten robes, it was lightweight, it did not require ironing, and everyone found the color acceptable. The alternative was quickly forgotten, and everyone came to agree that blue was the appropriate shade for the coven.

After purchasing the fabric and thread, and ropes for the belts, we returned to Arachne and Gabriel's home to begin the process of making robes. Everyone worked together to ensure that the robes were all cut and ready to be sewn. In the first afternoon and evening, half the robes were completed. The rest were finished over the next week. As I had never learned to use a sewing machine, Gabriel and Steve made my ritual robe, clearly enjoying the obvious gender reversal of doing the sewing for a woman. The blue robe remained an emblem of the coven; new initiates were required to make one when they joined the Circle of Light.

The process of traveling to the fabric store, choosing the fabric, and spending the day cutting and sewing the robes was an element of the cocooning in the coven. There was a growing interest and demand among the members to spend time together. Although not all of the weekends were filled with coven activities, an increasing number of Saturdays and Sundays were spent on coven events or with other coven members. Some of these involved doing rituals with other groups, going into the woods to perform rituals, or getting in touch with nature. Oscar, a film buff, began a Saturday night horror film showing in his home. Many coven members, their friends, as well as other people in the Neo-Pagan community stopped by to watch the movies, laugh, and play.

Intimacy was further encouraged by people's staying after each meeting, class, or ritual to eat and chat. Eating after a ritual or magical working is believed to ground the individual or bring her or him back to mundane life. However, it is also part of the work of intimacy, as people stayed longer and had a chance to discuss mundane as well as spiritual or magical issues. Every six weeks, after a sabbat, a new "goodies list" was created, to determine who was responsible for food and drinks for each meeting. Unlike the food at festivals, the snacks served after a class or meeting were not elaborate. Bagels and spreads served with soda or fruit juice were the most common fare. Every month we each contributed five dollars to a general fund, which supplied candles and incense for rituals and paper goods for feasts and after-class dining. The role of treasurer rotated every year among those willing to take on the responsibility. At the end of all classes, meetings, and rituals everyone hugged and kissed each other goodbye. In my fieldnotes I remarked that the show of affection was ritualized, almost pro forma. However, I came to realize that, as with the process of checking in, intimacy was being created.

Part of both the growing intimacy and the desire to be known as a group was displayed in the decision to request to be housed together during Rites of Spring, an EarthSpirit Community activity. Rites, the usual abbreviation for the festival, takes place every year at the end of May in a children's summer camp prior to its opening for the session. Rites is an intense time in which people live and eat together, participate in rituals, teach and participate in classes, and socialize. Hundreds of Neo-Pagans come together from throughout the United States, although most participants are drawn from the eastern seaboard. People who request and pay for housing are assigned a bunk; groups often ask to be placed in the same bunkhouse, and if possible the request is honored. Those who do not reserve a bunk can pitch a tent on the grounds for a smaller fee. Covens attending the festival together, either sharing a bunkhouse or an area in the campgrounds, frequently put up decorations—such as banners—that define the space as belonging to that group. The sharing of a bunkhouse by Circle of Light members was at once a sign in the larger community of Neo-Pagans of the spawning of a new coven and a commitment to live together in close quarters for five days.

Sharing a cramped living space simultaneously helped the group become closer and foreshadowed difficulties that would ultimately lead to rifts. Tempers flared during the week as we became painfully aware of differences in personal habits. Beth, a night owl, annoyed several members of the coven by coming in late at night, turning on the light, and making noise. We learned that some coven members snored loudly, and that others were messy—they left their personal possessions on their own and other's bunks. We also became aware of each other's generosity when we shared supplies brought from home that were not otherwise available on the camp site. Either all together or in groups of two, three, or four, coven members went to rituals, classes, and the dining hall, or sat or danced around the ritual fire. Coven members turned to one another when they became burned out from the intensity of the interactions or magical workings at the gathering. The shared experiences at Rites were part of the group's collective memory, which was alluded to in jokes and conversation long after we returned to Boston. However, some of the differences in personal habits and personalities that became apparent during that week ultimately led to tensions within the group. These, in turn, resulted in some departures from the coven within the next months or year. Nonetheless, the immediate response upon returning from Rites was a growing sense of the coven as a *family*—a group of people one could rely on even if some of their personal habits were annoying.

LEARNING WICCA

After the initial set of meetings to determine the organization of the coven, we began to meet weekly for classes. These classes, taught mostly by the elders, involved both magical teachings and discussion of the esabats and sabbats. Much of what was covered in the classes could be learned from books or from classes at occult bookstores. For instance, in one class we learned about the concept of the younger self, a well-established concept within Wiccan circles. The younger self is believed to be the child-like part of each of us that is not rational or linear in its thinking. It is more open to mystical experiences and to suggestions. The younger self tends, we were told by Gabriel, to take statements literally. It is for this reason that we should all avoid making statements that are negating of ourselves or others, such as "You are a clumsy or stupid person." Positive statements, particularly when made by the person herself or himself, are readily heard by the younger self.

We were each advised to write an affirmation that we would repeat daily for two weeks. The affirmation was part of the process of creating and recreating the self, as discussed in chapter 2. In a sentence or two, we were to state something positive about ourselves that we would repeat twice a day in front of the mirror. The affirmation was to involve an area in which we were uncertain or afraid. For example, if a man wanted to begin an art project but had been told in the past that he had little artistic ability, he would write an affirmation such as, "I am a good artist who will produce beautiful paintings and drawings."

Much of what we were taught can be found in a number of books. Starhawk (1979), for instance, discusses the younger self and its use in ritual. A number of writers, both within Wicca and from a more general popular psychological perspective, advocate having individuals do affirmations. However, the import of the class was not lessened by the fact that the information could have been obtained elsewhere. People were encouraged to participate in the activity because it was being done by the entire group. The process of talking about and doing it with others helped to legitimize the process. It was part of the cocooning through which people supported each other in learning and accepting behaviors and beliefs that are not universally accepted. The coven socializes the neophyte into the role of *Witch* in a way that merely reading about the magical religious traditions would not. The group helps to confer and confirm the neophyte's self-identity as a Witch. Furthermore, by being trained in a coven, the participants are placed within a network of people who have been trained by, or have practiced or participated in, the same coven, or perhaps one it hived from or one that hived from it.

The neophytes in the Circle of Light coven were required to keep a journal and to begin their own Book of Shadows. The journal was a record of their personal journey in the coven. People chronicled their attempts to do exercises, such as the affirmation, responses to readings, and classes. The elders in the coven required that the neophytes read the standard texts in Wicca, such as Starhawk (1979, 1982), Adler (1979, 1986), and certain novels that are popular within the community. The readings not only provided some of the training, teaching the participants about the mystical, mythical, and magical elements of the religion, but it also familiarized them with the language, poetry, and readings that are widespread within the community. In other words, the neophytes were being integrated into the larger community. Oscar and Linda, in the coven they began and in which they are high priest and priestess, insist that neophytes participate in some rituals and events of other covens and groups. Although this was not a requirement in the Circle of Light coven, we were as a group invited to participate in the coven in which Gabriel had trained, and to participate in other groups' rituals. This, like the required readings, provided an avenue to become connected with people in the larger Neo-Pagan community.

Witches in their Book of Shadows keep a handwritten copy of rituals for sabbats and esabats, as well as magical workings, poems, and chants. Each group I have attended has a slightly different way of casting the circle or calling in the quarters. During the year and a day that initiates were studying for their first degree in the Circle of Light coven, they were required to memorize the words for the casting of the circle, the calling of the quarters, and the Witch's Rune, a poem that is always recited by this group at the beginning of rituals. The time commitment necessary for memorization and writing the rituals in their Book of Shadows was significant—requiring that the coven and its work become central for the participants. The words of the rituals took on particular importance as they were repeated over and over again.

Secrecy

Secrecy is stressed within covens. In the Circle of Light coven we were all enjoined not to share the details of one another's lives or of rituals with people outside the group. McGuire (1994) and Neitz (1994), both relying on Simmel's work (1906), suggest that secrecy helps to create group cohesion, as an in-group and an out-group are created. Furthermore, secret societies permit their members to participate in activities considered unacceptable by the larger society. Although I was consistently treated as a friend, coven members were aware of my role as researcher. They were at times guarded about speaking openly in front of me. I had been excluded from some classes, the initiation rituals of members to their first degree, and some other rituals—I was told that as I was not myself becoming an initiated Witch, it would be either inappropriate or dangerous for me to witness the rites or participate in the classes. My participation in most rituals and classes—and my exclusion from some—helped to define my role as neither quite an insider nor an outsider. The secrecy was also important for the development of trust. The sense of feeling secure that one's secrets will not be repeated, nor will one's behavior be ridiculed, is an important element in feeling safe enough to become open with others.

Both McGuire (1994) and Neitz (1994) suggest that the use of secrecy is more consistent with male lodges or quasi-religions, which emphasize hierarchy and status, than with women's, particularly feminist spirituality groups. Wiccan covens are more hierarchical in structure than Dianic or other all-women's groups. Status differences exist in accordance with the degree or rank that different members have reached. Although all-women's groups do not have different degrees, within any group certain women are more likely to actually act as the leaders, either due to their greater knowledge or stronger personality. In practice the distinction between *power to* and *power over* is sometimes blurred, in both all-women's and inclusive groups. The lack of formal ranks within the Dianic groups is a direct outgrowth of adherence to feminist principles. However, within Wiccan groups that I have participated in, the role of the high priestess is accorded greater power than that of high priest. Although women participating in these groups are accepting a hierarchal relationship, with some members viewed as elders, the hierarchy is not one that favors the men over the women. The degrees or status become rationalized as related to knowledge and therefore viewed as a useful distinction. The differences in status, however, do result in tensions.

JUST LIKE A FAMILY

The coven is, in many ways, *just like a family*—filled with caring and concern and also with internal tensions and power struggles. Linda recently told me that being a high priestess is like being a mother to people who are your own age or older. "It is weird," she laughingly related, "to have a forty-year-old woman enter a coven meeting and say "Hi, Mom." Gabriel, who was high priest of the Circle of Light coven for nine and a half years, contended that having some knowledge of group dynamics and psychology would be very helpful in running a coven. Everyone comes into the group, he suggested, with many old wounds and hang-ups from their family background that are acted out in the coven.

Shortly after I stopped actively participating in the Circle of Light coven, Beth became ill. The coven members gathered around her to help her through the crisis. Arachne went with her to the hospital and stayed with her. All the coven members participated in her care after she left the hospital. Similarly, when anyone in the coven was ill or had a problem, all the members helped the person. Magical rites to send energy for healing were always done, but so were the mundane jobs—picking up food, doing laundry, and helping clean the person's apartment.

Existing alongside this group support, however, was the growth of tensions among members—which ultimately resulted in the high turnover in membership within the coven. Some tensions developed immediately. Barry never seemed to fit into the group and left within the first year. Coven members complained that he sang out of tune and too loud. While these complaints were true, I took them as metaphors for his failing to make friends with the other coven members. Beth had commented that he always seemed down and never had any positive news when we checked in. My fieldnotes on the comments made during the check-in period do not reveal his comments to have been more consistently negative than the average. As Stark and Bainbridge (1985) noted, "Objectively trivial individual habits and matters of taste often are extremely salient for personal relationships" (326). It is hard to pinpoint why Barry did not fit in, but clearly from the beginning his sense of humor and his way of playing and even of presenting his troubles were different. He was gently asked to leave by Arachne and Gabriel, although officially it was presented as a mutual decision.

Gail, one of the initial elders, had become more and more alienated. She left after the first year, for three main reasons. First, she felt isolated as three couples formed in the coven. Second, she was older than the other participants and felt her needs and concerns were somewhat different. Third, her main link to the coven was through Arachne, who during the first year became closer to Beth.

Linda and Oscar stayed with the group to receive their second degrees. They left to create their own coven after Arachne and Gabriel moved to a rural area more than an hour's drive from the center of town. Although at one time the two couples had been very close friends, living in apartments near one another and spending much of their free time together, their relationship has cooled. Tensions apparently formed around the issues of training and of the new coven's obligation to the one that trained its founders. Beth broke from the coven shortly after getting well but then reappeared a few years later. As personality conflicts and disputes over training, classes, and authority grew, the old group disintegrated. Arachne and Gabriel's move from the center of town signaled the breakdown of the original group. New people joined and had their own effect on the group.

Oddly, it was the intensity of the relationships—similar to those in modern marriages and families—that resulted in the splits. Friendships, like all intimate relationships in modernity, are fragile, based on shared interests and intimacy, but not anchored in economic or political necessity. As in families, however, peculiar recombinations and reconciliations occur. Steve and Carol, who left the coven when tension developed between Steve and one of the other men, returned to rituals at the Circle of Light several years ago. The coven changed but, until it folded at the fall equinox, it still drew old members together. Links continued between members who remained in the coven and those who left. Although covens remain fluid, with membership fluctuating, rifts occurring, and possibly the coven itself falling apart, the primary relationships of the coven continue to call to its participants. Recombinations of some of the same people occur. New covens grow out of the cinders of the old. Much like modern families, the covens are reconstituted—forming odd family trees.

At the end of all rituals at the Circle of Light coven, as well as at several other groups I have attended, everyone joins hands and chants, "Merry meet, Merry part, and Merry meet again." Although the parting of members from a coven is frequently acrimonious, fissures heal and old coven mates come back together to celebrate sabbats, work together magically, or form into a coven again. Covens and coven membership fluctuate, but the relationships formed in the crucible of the coven remain important to the participants and within the workings of the larger Neo-Pagan community.

High priestess doing incantation during handfasting (marriage) ritual. (Photograph by author)

High priestess joining together the hands of the bride and groom at a handfasting. (Photograph by author)

High priest in ritual
robes. (Photograph by
author)

Witch in ritual robes.
(Photograph by author)

Ritual altar. (Photograph by author)

North altar at Circle of Light coven's 1996 Beltane ritual.
(Photograph by author)

Bumper sticker with the Neo-Pagan symbol of the pentagram. (Photograph by author)

CHAPTER 4

A Circle within a Circle

The Neo-Pagan Community

> We are all longing to go home to some place we have never
> been—a place, half-remembered, and half-envisioned we can
> only catch glimpses of from time to time. Community.
> Somewhere, there are people to whom we can speak with
> passion without having the words catch in our throats.
> Somewhere a circle of hands will open to receive us, eyes will
> light up as we enter, voices will celebrate with us whenever
> we come into our own power. Community means strength
> that joins our strength to do the work that needs to be done.
>
> (Starhawk 1982:92)

The notion of community permeates the way Neo-Pagans and
Witches speak about their religion. Writing about the death of a friend
and member of her coven, one woman states, "We [the coven members]
assembled together to . . . plan a public memorial service which would
include Jody's family, the Pagan community, the gay community who all
mourned him" (D. N. Arthen 1990:5). The term *community* calls to mind
for many a romantic portrayal of life in a small town where everyone
knows and cares for one another (Wrong 1976:77). This nostalgic image
of community has resonance in Witches' more general romanticization of
a previous era—a time when life was simpler, the needs of all people were
met, and nature was revered.

George Hillery (1955) counts ninety-four different definitions of community in the sociological literature. The only factor these definitions share
is that they involve people. The term *community*, as it is used among Neo-
Pagans, often has two meanings. For example, in the article entitled "From

they *become* microcosms of their communities, and their communities change with their entrance" (87).

All communities, even traditional ones, involve people who differ from one another to some degree. Community "does not clone behavior or ideas. It is a commonality of *forms* (ways of behaving) whose content (meanings) may vary considerably among its members. The triumph of community is to so contain this variety that its inherent discordance does not subvert the apparent coherence which is expressed by its boundaries" (Cohen 1985:20). Differences among participants are probably greater in communities of choice, which may be one of several groups or communities the individual belongs to, than in communities of birth and geography. However, it is a mistake to view any community as monolithic. A number of feminist writers (for example, Friedman 1995; Weiss 1995; Held 1995) criticize communitarian theory for its emphasis on the community as formative of the individual to the exclusion of a recognition of differences that exist among members.

Phelan (1995), while acknowledging the diversity of the lesbian community, argues that it participates in four processes that define it as a community. First, it provides a place that lesbians can be insulated from hostility to their sexual orientation. Second, it furnishes an escape for lesbians from invisibility in the larger community. Third, it supplies models for creating a lesbian persona, helping entrants interpret (or reinterpret) their lives. Fourth, it furnishes an avenue for political activity (87–88).

Phelan's model of lesbian communities also applies to Neo-Pagans. Similarly to homosexuals, Witches and Neo-Pagans frequently feel that the larger social world is hostile to them. Witches, appropriating the concept from the homosexual community, speak of coming out of the broom closet. Witches, like homosexuals, fear—often with good cause—that their "coming out" will have negative repercussions for them, ranging from rejection by family and friends to difficulties at work. Both lesbians and Witches are marginal groups within the culture; their members often keep their identity hidden.

All four of the processes described by Phelan for the construction of a lesbian community are applicable to Neo-Pagans. The Neo-Pagan community provides a nonhostile environment in which members of this religion can become visible. At Neo-Pagan gatherings people openly dress in ritual robes and jewelry. People seem to be flaunting their religious affiliation, in part because it is normally hidden or deemphasized. The community provides modeling, teaching new members rituals, magical practices, and ways to interpret or reinterpret their lives. For example, through participation in the Neo-Pagan community they come to see their lives as guided by the forces of nature or the goddesses. Neo-Pagans like lesbians and gay men are involved in life politics. Lesbians' concerns surround acceptance of their sexual orientation; Witches, through their participation in an earth-based, feminist religion, embrace both feminist and ecological concerns.

Both the Neo-Pagan and homosexual communities have permeable boundaries. People may be considered members who do not have face-to-face interactions and who, in fact, do not know one another. Both communities involve people who are dissimilar from one another in many of their beliefs and practices.

It is hard to speak of Witches as a community of believers, as some subgroups within Neo-Paganism are feminist separatists, while others exalt the male aspect as well as the feminine. However, as discussed in chapter 1, Neo-Pagans do share a number of beliefs and practices. Although traditions or varieties of practice and belief differ, the rituals are similar enough that a person from one tradition would feel comfortable at the rituals of a coven of a different tradition. On one occasion a visitor from the West Coast was invited to a sabbat ritual at the Circle of Light coven. He had learned about and contacted the coven through a Neo-Pagan magazine after he realized that he would be away on business during his coven's sabbat celebration. Although he knew no one in the group, he was made welcome. He seemed quite comfortable during the ritual. Afterward he spoke of the differences between the ceremony he had just participated in and those of his own coven. He claimed that he was struck by certain powerful aspects of the ritual he had participated in, aspects that he hoped to have his own coven adopt. Clearly the differences he witnessed did not make him feel alienated from the ritual.

Although no one dogma or set of practices is universal among Neo-Pagans, there is enough similarity among groups to suggest the existence of Shutz's (1964) "shared life world." The acceptance of a magical, mystical worldview, as well as the participation in Wiccan rituals, creates this shared life world. Within Wiccan circles people normally speak of being guided by the goddess or of making life decisions based on reading the tarot. The notion that trees, animals, and inanimate objects have a spirit with which one can communicate and gain power is regularly accepted. Although not all Wiccans agree with any one or all of these propositions, their pervasiveness within the community provides a shared set of assumptions. The chants, music, and dance, as well the similarity of the basic components of ritual, provide continuity among groups. The sharing of ritual participation—and more importantly of ecstatic states in which one *experiences* the goddess or the forces of the universe—is important in the formation of a shared life world.

At the end of *Habits of the Heart* (1985), Bellah et al. call for the renewal of community: "They [the people interviewed] realize that though the processes of separation and individuation were necessary to free us from the tyrannical structures of the past, they must be balanced by a renewal of commitment and community if they are not to end in self-destruction or turn into their opposites" (277). This new community, according to Bellah et al., cannot recapture the small town of yesterday; instead this new community might be based on a reappropriation of the biblical and republican traditions on which small towns were based (283). Clearly, lesbian and Neo-Pagan communities are challenging the biblical if not the republican traditions of "small-town America." Bellah et al. would view both lesbians and Neo-Pagans as contributing to the fracturing of stereotypical American culture. But these groups may, nonetheless, provide one model of a new community—one based not on shared geography, but on a shared life world. In this life world, in the term used by Bellah et al., a "community of memory" is formed, one in which exemplary women and men are celebrated and there is a sense of a shared history.

COMMUNITY OF MEMORY

A community of memory is created, according to Bellah et al., through the recounting of the group's past glories, its troubles, the injustices it has sustained, and those it has committed against others. Through the telling and retelling of the narrative of its past and of the men and women who are exemplars of its glory, group cohesion develops. Bellah et al. argue that to be a real community is to share a history. They illustrate the community of memory through an interviewee, Ruth Levy. She describes her own recognition of her membership in the Jewish community after noticing a number tattooed on the arm of another woman.

The notion of the Holocaust as a symbol that helps to shape a community is more fully developed by Rapaport (1997), who studied contemporary German Jews. Many of the people interviewed by Rapaport were not religious, but nonetheless they defined themselves ethnically, if not religiously, as Jews. Rapaport notes that both the collective memory of the Holocaust and biblical stories of disaster, such as the destruction of the first temple or the expulsion from Egypt, are important in establishing a sense of community. An illusory *us* and *them* are constructed through these memories, which help to create and sustain the boundaries of the community.

Rapaport reminds us that the memory of past events is always negotiated; those who have the power determine which aspects of the past will be recalled and which subverted. The collective memory of any group will continue only as long as past events are commemorated, either by descendants of the original group or others who claim the history. The past must be understood as constructed in the present as a way of creating an image of the future. Rapaport notes, "The Holocaust provides the framework for representing the past, understanding the present, and envisioning the future. It is their [the respondents'] ultimate metaphor, a part of their roots, the source from which the meanings they bestow to daily life are constituted" (Rapaport 1997:12).

The community of memory for Witches is more openly and clearly constructed than that of the Holocaust for Jews. Many Witches acknowledge that they are not the direct descendants of the victims, primarily women who were executed as Witches in the early modern period. Nonetheless, the witch trials remain symbolically important to help unify a diverse group of people from different ethnic and religious backgrounds. The trials provide a historic period of martyrdom, similar to the Holocaust for Jews. The cry "Never Again the Burning Times" is equivalent to the slogan "We Will Never Forget," which is associated with commemorating the Holocaust. Some Witches claim to be either direct descendants of those executed in the trials,[2] or to have themselves been victims of the witch craze in a previous life.[3] Most Witches, however, see the link as symbolic—between themselves and people who, like them, participated in an ancient religion; were folk healers, magicians, or women of power; or who just practiced the "old ways."

Starhawk (1982) suggests that the trials were an attack on the old religion by the Christian church, on women healers and midwives by the medical profession, and on women whose bodies were viewed as both a site of immanence and of sexuality by a new antisexual ideology. By symbolically linking themselves to the historic witches, present-day Witches are helping to define their present and future. They are identifying with those they define as victims of the church, the modern medical establishment, and an ideology that degrades women and sexuality. Alternatively Witches are defining themselves as returning to a more nature-based, less hierarchal religion—one that honors immanence in nature and in women's and men's bodies. It is a religion that celebrates sexuality as a positive life-affirming force. The witch trials and their victims become a metaphor for the destruction of an alternative society—one in which, the Witches claim, people lived in harmony with nature and one another. In this society women had a central role, as wise women and as healers.

The witch trials, as well as the image of the society that preceded them—a pre-industrial bucolic life, in which nature and women were honored—provide a mythology for the creation of a modern community. The fact that the links between present-day Witches and the historic victims of the trials are figurative does not delegitimize the import of this history for the creation of community. Cohen (1985) notes that all groups reconstruct their histories, in relationship to present issues and problems. Although Witches create their history more self-consciously than the people of traditional communities that Cohen studies, the process is not significantly different. Cohen, like Rapaport, reminds us that the construction of a historic past, or mythology, is used by groups to negotiate the present. This mythology provides models of behavior, of responses to adversity, and of a sense of community. Witches are modern, well-educated people who are self-consciously developing a mythology of the past. The symbolic creation aligns with the life-political issues of contemporary Witches—ecological issues, women's issues, and those of remystifying the world. The community created by Witches, like all communities, constructs a past that is applicable to their present and that helps them create a future.

COMMUNITY BUILDING

Festivals are the most visible way that Neo-Pagans build a community. About sixty festivals, involving between forty and a thousand people, are held throughout the United States each year (Pike 1996:123). The gatherings usually take place in a rural area for a period of a weekend to a week, although some of the earliest festivals in the late 1960s and early 1970s were held in hotels (Adler 1986:422–23). Festivals provide an opportunity for people to gather from around the country and sometimes from other countries to meet, exchange ideas, practice rituals, sing songs, have fun, and feel part of an ongoing community. Festivals are very emotionally and socially intense events, as people live in confined, often crowded spaces with shared bathrooms, kitchens, and sleeping spaces. Gatherings can be either for men and women or unisex. Among the single-sex gatherings, those for women are the more numerous.

When I go to a gathering, I am always struck by the feeling of entering a different world. There is an air of returning to summer camp as an adult. This sensation is strengthened by the summer-camp settings of both

EarthSpirit Community festivals, Rites of Spring and Twilight Covening; however, the feeling is less due to the facilities than the fact that the group of people have gathered during their leisure time to play, learn, and live together. Women and men, many of whom in their mundane lives work in traditional jobs where they dress conservatively, are now clearly "off-duty." People wander the dirt lanes in a variety of outfits. Some wear ritual robes, cloaks, and medieval attire, while others are naked or seminaked. There are men wearing skirts and makeup, as well as men and women dressed in blue jeans and T-shirts. The initial encounter is visually overwhelming.

At large gatherings the campsite is set up as a village, with the dining hall, meeting places, and vendors at the center of the camp. The vendors sell objects that would be appealing to members of this group—velvet capes, tarot cards, velvet or silken pouches to hold amulets, books, herbs and crystals for healing and good luck, silver jewelry, and beads. They also offer body painting and massages. Some of the vendors are businesspeople who cater to Wiccan, New Age, or general occult audiences, although the majority are Neo-Pagans who use the sales to help pay their expenses at the festival. Festival organizers usually collect a fee from the vendors and sometimes a percentage of the earnings. While some gatherings exclude vendors, on the whole they are welcome, as they help to defray festival costs, and they add to the village atmosphere. The vendors' stands often become a center of activity, as people cluster around the area looking at handmade objects or those with magical significance.

At most festivals there is a dining area or hall, where people communally prepare and share food. At Rites of Spring, as at most of the festivals, the organizers provide the food and a skeleton kitchen staff. At some festivals people do their own cooking at their campsites, but this is more the exception than the rule; the sharing of food—preparing meals and sitting down together—is an important part of creating a village atmosphere. During meals people sit at long tables, talking to old friends and making new ones. It is a time in which people make contacts, both for spiritual and magical workings and for more mundane concerns such as the availability of apartments and postdoctoral fellowships. In between meals people often use the tables and benches as a quiet spot to sit, write, draw, or talk to a friend.

In part to save costs, and in part to reinforce the ideology of belonging to a Pagan community, people are expected to volunteer at all gatherings for work assignments. Everyone who participates in the meal plan is expected to help either prepare or clean-up after one meal. In addition, participants are asked to volunteer for another activity, such as taking care of children, lifeguarding at a lake or pool, working in the healers' hut, or directing the parking of cars. There are always some people who do not meet their obligations, so that others must do extra work. Although Neo-Pagans tend to share a laissez-faire attitude tensions can mount as a group of people try to live together. Individuals not meeting their work obligations, taking frequent and long showers when hot water and facilities are limited, throwing cigarette butts in the ritual fire, being loud late at night or early in the morning in areas where others are sleeping—all these activities can increase tensions. Because festivals last only a few days or at most a week, the problems do not become full-blown. On the whole, people do not leave the festivals remembering the annoying aspects of group living. Instead they focus on the "magical energy" that they have felt at the festivals, the joy of seeing old friends, meeting some new people, and exchanging ideas and gossip with others in the community.

The magical atmosphere that many Neo-Pagans experience at festivals is created through the large number of rituals, magical activities, and workshops that occur in a very condensed time span. Ritual circles celebrate the rising of the sun and the moon, the gathering of the tribes, the beginning of a new day on the campsite, and the festival itself. Circles of recovery for individuals who were drug or alcohol dependent, as well as all-women's or all-men's circles, are regularly organized. It is not uncommon for a person to participate in two or three rituals in a day. At the larger festivals, where people of many different traditions gather, preparing a ritual provides an avenue for groups to display their particular practices to the larger community. Covens can also participate in cross-fertilizing each others' practices.

The development of a unified body of knowledge is also facilitated through the workshops. People who want to share their knowledge or techniques lead workshops on standard topics such as astral projection, writing rituals, drumming, ritual dance, song, crystal magic, and healing through herbs. Some workshops are organized to discuss a topic of interest or concern, such as how to raise a Pagan child in the mundane world, coming out of the broom closet to your family and friends, Witches and technology, or the feasibility of creating an ongoing Pagan village or living site. Dialogues begun at these workshops are often discussed further in journals and newsletters and on the Internet.

Ritual fires are lit and sustained throughout many festivals. They are often the center of activity at night, when people gather around to drum, dance, or watch. The beat starts to pick up as the evening proceeds.

An outer ring of people watches as men and women dance nude or partially dressed in front of the fire. Dancers sway in a sort of trance to the beat of the drum, or dance in swirling motions around the fire.[4] Some people, mostly those in their twenties, stay up all night dancing and drumming. Liaisons are made at the campfire, some of which last for the night, or for the festival; some become long-term relationships. There are conflicts concerning appropriate behavior around the ritual fire. Some women have complained that while dancing naked or seminaked around the fire they felt their personal space invaded and their safety threatened by men who have made sexual advances (Pike 1996:135–38; A. Arthen 1992). A party atmosphere sometimes develops around the fire, in conflict with the notion of it as a sacred space. Nonetheless, the fire, the dancing, and the drumming are important aspects of the transformative, magical power of festivals. The ritual fire provides a place for people to meditate and to pursue their own spiritual quests while in the company of others. Some people learn to drum while sitting around the fire, or they explore ecstatic dance.

Even with the conflicts that develop, the festivals are viewed by Neo-Pagans as models for the development of Neo-Pagan community life. Margot Adler notes that after attending the Michigan Women's Music festival, she felt affirmed in her religion, because as she describes it, Paganism was the "state religion" at the festival. The songs, chants, and rituals were Neo-Pagan in their orientation. She noted that she had never before been in a small city where she felt so visible and accepted as a Witch (Adler 1992:23). The process of going to festivals is the same for many Neo-Pagans. They often live and work in communities in which their religious affiliation is either not known or is considered an oddity. They therefore enjoy being in a group in which they are practicing the "state religion" even for a short time.

The festivals are part of the process through which Neo-Pagans form networks, meet one another, learn new chants, and share magical practices. They provide an arena in which information about Neo-Paganism can flourish and spread. In "The Pagan Census" we found that 42 percent had attended one or more festivals that year; 57.1 percent of the respondents had not attended a festival in the preceding year; 0.9 percent did not respond to this question (H. Berger et al. n.d.). Our survey suggests that a larger proportion of Neo-Pagans attend festivals than Adler estimated (1986). Based on her sense of the Neo-Pagan community, she suggested that approximately 10 percent of Neo-Pagans attend festivals. The difference between our findings and Adler's estimate may be a changing pattern of attendance among Neo-Pagans in the last decade, an underestimate on her part, or the result of our sample being skewed because it was not randomly distributed. However, regardless of the exact percentage of Neo-Pagans who attend festivals, there is little doubt that festivals create community. Even though she believes only a small percentage of people attend festivals, Adler argues that these events are helping to change the face of Neo-Paganism. She notes that those who do attend bring back information about available resources, rituals, and magical practices to their covens and to other Pagans in their locality. The festivals also provide Neo-Pagans with a vision of what a Pagan community might be like—resulting in the development of images of alternative communities and attempts by some groups to buy land to create those communities.

Whether or not Neo-Pagans attend festivals, they participate in the larger community by reading books and journals. Starhawk and Adler are the two most influential authors, although other Witches have also reached celebrity status through their writings and by organizing festivals. Neo-Pagans emphasize that they themselves help to create and reinterpret rituals; however, they are influenced by the books and journals that they read. Through reading the same books, people come to share a life world in which the terms of discourse, the way covens are organized, and the way rituals are enacted become increasingly similar. For example, as was shown in chapter 3, the Circle of Light coven used Starhawk's suggestion of having a facilitator at meetings, her notion of a higher self, and her phrase "the coven is a place of perfect love and perfect trust" to describe their aspirations for their group.

The use of desktop publishing and the Internet have made this an interactive national community, even if not always on a face-to-face basis. As was noted in chapter 1, because it is relatively easy to set up a journal, over a hundred Neo-Pagan journals presently exist. Individuals frequently write in to newsletters to raise concerns, disagree with articles, or respond to letters in previous issues. Some of the newsletters are local; others have subscribers throughout the United States.

There are also a growing number of Neo-Pagan, Wiccan, and women's spirituality sites on the Internet. Even more directly than newsletters, this medium provides a venue for people to exchange ideas, make contacts, and learn about the resources within the larger community. As with festivals, the importance of the Internet's impact does not depend on the direct participation of all Neo-Pagans. Linda, who had access to the Internet through her computer at work, often mentioned current online debates at the Circle of Light coven meetings. This would in turn stimulate discussion at the coven, some of which she then posted on the Internet.

On a local level, open rituals bring people together in large numbers. Some of the larger sabbat rituals—which take place in state parks, rented space from Unitarian Universalist churches, or occult bookstores, among other places—can involve more than a hundred people. Even those rituals that occur in people's homes can be attended by thirty to forty people packed into living rooms, basements, and backyards. Open rituals, like large festivals, provide a milieu in which friendships are formed and maintained, people's participation in this new religion is affirmed, and neophytes learn about the process of becoming a Witch. They help create a network of local people who become integrated into each others' lives on several levels—couples meet and people exchange information and just have fun together.

Occult bookstores, particularly those owned and operated by Witches, often serve as a stable local center. These stores typically provide classes in tarot reading, creation of ritual, drumming, astral projection, or aspects of magical practice. The classroom space is used for open sabbat and esabat rituals. Information about the formation of a new coven or a request for a ride to a festival are posted around the store or on a bulletin board. People drop by to shop, visit with the owner or store workers, and meet one another. The stores become part of the larger network through which Pagans in the same area see old friends and meet new people.

Although the community of Witches is amorphous, it nonetheless is a community, one that exists on both a national and local level. Participants' degree of involvement can range from daily interactions to no face-to-face contact. It is a community in which there are disagreements and power struggles. Nonetheless, a community of interest, of concern, and of a shared life world is created.

Emancipatory Politics/Life Politics

Shane Phelan notes that the lesbian community is formed in part through providing an avenue for political activity (1995). Lesbians and gay men have been actively fighting for their rights since the late 1960s. Some Witches have also organized to ensure that their civil rights will not be truncated. For example, Laurie Cabot and other members of her coven in Salem, Massachusetts, created the Witches' Anti-Defamation League to defend the rights of Witches. The league won the right to place in the Witches' Museum in Salem a plaque stating that neither the victims of the witch craze nor modern-day practitioners of Witchcraft are Satan worshippers or evildoers. Members of this group protest films that have negatively portrayed Witches, such as *The Witches of Eastwick;* and they organize political protests and legal actions in support of Witches who believe they are suffering from discrimination on the job, in housing, or in court custody cases. The Witches' Anti-Defamation League is one of a number of organizations that have organized protests and letter-writing campaigns to stop negative stereotyping and discrimination against Witches.

Although Witches are concerned about negative publicity and discrimination, these issues are not the core of their political activity. Issues of gender equality, environmental responsibility, and gay and lesbian rights tend to be more central. Witches vary in their political commitment. At one end of the spectrum are those who are only tangentially involved politically. At the other end are Witches, like Starhawk, who participate in demonstrations to close down nuclear power plants, to stop the despoliation of the earth, and to fight for economic justice and gender equality. When fighting for these issues, Witches join groups whose membership and leadership may not be composed primarily of Wiccans. However, Witches view their political commitment as an extension of their spirituality. As a thirty-six-year-old lesbian noted, "For me my spirituality/ politics/ sexuality all overlap. One is no good without the others" (H. Berger and A. Arthen n.d.:2523).

In joining political organizations, such as environmental groups, Witches and others are participating in what Giddens refers to as emancipatory politics. According to Giddens, emancipatory politics grew out of the Enlightenment of the eighteenth century, a movement that fought to break the shackles of tradition and religion. During this period the concept of the "rights of men" was first developed and the divine right of kings was questioned. The locus of emancipatory politics is the growth of autonomy for individuals. One strand of political activity that grew out of the development of the "rights of men" is the questioning of all forms of exploitation, inequality, and oppression. According to Giddens, emancipatory politics is based on a hierarchical notion of power in which "power is understood as the capability of an individual or group to exert its will over others" (Giddens 1991:211). This type of politics continues to be of import, but Giddens argues that late modernity has seen the rise of another type—life politics.

Life politics, the politics of choice, is an important component of the Wiccan community. I have attended many rituals whose focus, at least in part, was to help heal the earth. After participating in a ritual to send healing energy to the rain forest, I interviewed Doug, a mild-mannered man in his thirties who had received his Ph.D. in mathematics from the

University of Chicago. When I asked whether or not he thought that the ritual we had just participated in would help the rain forest, he responded,

> I think that the world is different than [it would have been] if these things [rituals] had not been done. If you get a bunch of people that do magical ritual together, they share some idea that is different than if they had all read the same book. They share an idea on some level that you don't get to by talking or reading a book or something. Having shared that idea, they do different things—and their actions are more coordinated somehow—even without their talking about it. And it is their actions that then change the world and they do different things then if they did not do this ritual. (Doug Interview 1988)

Although rituals involve a changing of the self, as discussed in chapter 2, ecological, feminist, and sexual-orientation issues are also important elements in rituals and in discussions within the Neo-Pagan community.

According to Giddens, "life politics concerns political issues which flow from processes of self-actualisation in post-traditional contexts, where globalising influences intrude deeply into the reflective project of the self, and conversely where the process of self-realisation influences global strategies" (1991:214). The women's movement, with its emphasis on changing the personal life trajectories, family relationships, and work patterns of women, is the clearest example of life politics. The notion of the personal and political as intertwined, however, has become integrated into many social movements of late modernity—for example, the environmental and the gay and lesbian movements (Melucci 1985). Life politics is not completely separated from emancipatory politics; however, it does incorporate a different notion of power—power as generative or transformative. Power to, as opposed to power over.

Life politics has been incorporated into Wicca. Whether or not individuals are actively involved in emancipatory politics, they are, through their participation in this new religious movement, involved in life politics. As Judy, a Gardnerian high priestess, states, "I always wanted to be a goddess worshipper because of the feminist and ecological implications" (Judy Interview 1987). To worship the goddess, for Witches, is to worship nature and the female aspect—to live a life that is consistent with the needs of the environment and to be aware of women's issues. Witches often speak of a sense of coming home when they find Wicca. One element of that sense of belonging is finding a spiritual expression that is consistent with their lifestyle concerns. Being part of a community that celebrates these concerns, in turn, increases each person's awareness of changes that are required in their lifestyle for them to live consistently with their principles. Being politically involved, furthermore, often is viewed as an element of living one's principles (Finley 1991; Starhawk 1991).

Participants in Wicca pride themselves on their tolerance of diverse lifestyles, interpretations of ritual, and beliefs. Wicca has no single moral code that all participants are required to follow. Raphael (1996) argues that this lack of a unified moral code, combined with the ambiguous status of the goddess as either existing within each woman (or person) or as a separate divine source, ultimately will result in the disintegration of the religion. "In the name of modern tolerance and self-realization, thealogy refuses to impose any authority (even feminist) on itself and is therefore subject to . . . fragmentation, relativization, and psychologization" (Raphael 1996:204). Although Raphael is criticizing feminist Witchcraft, or what I refer to as women's-only Witchcraft groups, the same appraisal could be made of integrated groups, who also do not rely on the existence of an *ultimate* authority or one interpretation of the goddess(es) or god(s).

According to Raphael, it is Witchcraft's late modern propensities, most particularly a hermeneutics of suspicion in which all truth claims—even its own—are questioned, that make it impossible for this religion to provide a unified moral code. She contrasts this with the more traditional religious expressions of Judaism and Christianity, which she believes do furnish their adherents with both a moral code and a source of comfort during times of sorrow or injustice. However, these religions developed prior to or in the early stages of modernity. It was in part the traditional authority of these religions that the Enlightenment thinkers rebelled against. In comparison, Wicca is a religion of late modernity. It therefore has incorporated skepticism about all knowledge and beliefs. Postmodern theorists have argued that truth claims and by extension moral codes are at best locally constituted and specific to a particular community (Rosenau 1992:77). Giddens, however, suggests that although the death of grand narratives has eliminated the traditional justification of moral codes, there is a reembedding of moral issues as an outgrowth of life politics. Women's issues, gay rights, and ecological concerns all "demand a renewed sensitivity to questions that institutions of modernity systematically dissolve" (1991:224).

There is a reembedding of moral issues occurring in Wicca; however, in this religion of late modernity the process is by necessity different from that in religions that developed prior to or in early modernity. As Margot Adler asserts, "The Craft has given me a rock-bottom set of values that I think are incredibly important. Those values have to do with diversity and multiplicity and freedom. They have to do with your view of yourself—your view of your body, your mind, your sexuality" (1992:27). Within the context of a liberal acceptance of differences and a recognition of the disintegration of a single moral basis for the creation of a universal ethical system, there is nonetheless the development of a value system— one based on mutual tolerance, concern for equity among people, and respect for the environment. Within Wicca issues of living in a manner that is consistent with maintenance of the global ecosystem, and that supports gender equality and the rights of others, are embedded in the rituals, chants, and concerns of the participants. It is a moral system in the making—which will never have the ultimate set of rules and regulations that exists in the religious and moral systems that developed in earlier eras. It does, however, provide a form of political and moral life that helps to unify this community.

CHAPTER 5

The Next Generation

The main ritual at Rites of Spring was as usual delayed by the need to create intricate props and coordinate the efforts of an amateur crew. The organizers had put up makeshift dividers to block off the main field as they prepared the area for the ritual. Accustomed to operating on "Pagan Standard Time," people wandered into the woods, went for a walk to the lake, or milled around chatting until we were invited into the circle. A bell was rung and drumming begun to call everyone who wished to participate into the field. About two hundred people formed into an uneven, amoeba-like circle around a lilac-covered mound constructed to mimic the shape of a pregnant woman's swollen abdomen. It was a warm sunny day at the end of May and the aroma of the lilacs filled the air.

The drumming came to a halt as one of the organizers walked into the center of the group and welcomed us. She said that prior to the casting of the circle the children of the community would bless the circle in their own manner. Eleven children ranging in age from about three to ten years came into the field singing and ringing bells. The children were sandwiched between a man who was drumming to keep the beat and a woman following to look after all the stragglers. Everyone smiled as the children's thin voices were heard singing of mother earth, father sky, and the flowers in the garden. The children and their two adult attendants danced around the circle singing and then left for another area of the camp to play games as the ritual continued.

The ritual focused on fertility in nature and in the participants' lives. As the ritual was about to end, the womblike structure broke open, and out of it stepped a woman—naked, in her last trimester of pregnancy, wearing a garland of lilacs. A gasp could be heard around the circle as she ascended from the earth. She looked beautiful, full of life and expectancy. She was the symbol of the second face of the goddess—the mother—and of fecundity in life and nature. She and the children who graced the circle prior to its being cast also represent the changes that are occurring within the Neo-Pagan community as the next generation is born.

As the religion and its participants age, more and more children are being born to Neo-Pagan parents. In "The Pagan Census" 41.3 percent of our respondents stated that they have children, and only .02 percent did not answer this question (H. Berger et al. n.d.). I would estimate conservatively that more than 82,600 children are being raised in Neo-Pagan families throughout the United States.[1]

A bright twelve-year-old girl, commenting on growing up in a Neo-Pagan family, confided, "Well, in school it [being a Neo-Pagan] sort of does [affect me] 'cause it's dangerous—you can't say what you are—like if someone asks you your religion then you are in a tight spot" (Shara Mayfire Interview 1995). To protect Shara and their other two children, her parents have joined a local Unitarian Universalist church. Shara's mother, Bonnie, told me that the Unitarians are open enough to permit her and her husband to feel comfortable, while providing a religious affiliation for their children that is recognized by their conservative neighbors. Bonnie's children can openly speak about their participation in the Unitarian Universalist church, although they are careful not to mention the Neo-Pagan rituals that are practiced in their home or the festival the family attends each year.

When I asked Shara if she knew any other Neo-Pagan youngsters, she said she suspected that there may be others in the area, "but you know you can't ask them because if they're not [Neo-Pagan] you're in deep deep trouble" (Shara Mayfire Interview 1995). Her nine-year-old brother interjected, "You can ask them their religion but they are likely to do the same thing as you" (A. Mayfire Interview 1995). Some parents, like Shara's, are joining the Unitarian Universalist church so they and their children will have a socially acceptable religious affiliation.[2] Others have excluded their children from their religious practice, while still others are attempting to raise their children as practicing Neo-Pagans.

THE PLACE OF CHILDREN

The debate over the integration of children into the religion is occurring in the same venues as those used by Neo-Pagans to exchange ideas on how to run a coven or create a ritual—that is, in books, journal articles, and discussions on the Internet. Although no consensus has been reached, both the terms and language of the debate are defined within this literature. The debate goes to the heart of how the religion will be defined. A tension exists between the conception of the religion as a spiritual path or paths that each person can choose to join, and the "old religion" that unifies a community. The contradiction between the two conceptions of Wicca became apparent only as children were brought into the religion.

Neo-Pagans have expressed concerns about both the method and appropriateness of bringing children into this new religion. Writing in a Neo-Pagan journal, Michael Sontag voices his apprehension that the religion will become diluted if children are raised as Neo-Pagans and Witches. "By bringing people on to the magickal path, as opposed to them finding the path themselves, we run the risk of finding ourselves dealing with an increasingly apathetic magickal community" (Sontag 1994:13). Sontag worries that the Neo-Pagan community could eventually suffer from the same problems he perceives among organized religions—a preponderance of participants who are only nominally involved. He asserts that the community would be better served by focusing on the personal growth and initiation of spiritual seekers than by expending time training children. Although Sontag's misgivings about the effect of children on the religion are shared by others, these concerns are more often voiced by people who are childless. Most parents are more concerned about their children than the effect their children may have on the religion.

Neo-Pagan parents are anxious about their offspring having the same negative experiences they themselves endured as children when their parents forced them to attend religious services that bored them. They want their children to be free to develop their own spiritual interests. As one Neo-Pagan mother wrote, "When I think of the next generation, I do not think of it in terms of Pagan or Magick, but in terms of individuals each finding their own unique path through the world—no matter what that might be" (Stanford-Blake 1994:21). On the whole, Neo-Pagan parents support the notion of their children's following their own spiritual interests. Their child-rearing techniques reflect the ideology of openness and anti-authoritarianism that permeates this religion. However, like most parents, Neo-Pagans hope their children will develop in healthy and productive ways and have interests the parents can respect.

Holly Teague (1994), a Neo-Pagan mother who advocates that children be free to find their own spiritual path, described her experience with her daughter. Teague had initially taken her young daughter out into the woods to create a sacred circle. As children are believed to be more spiritually open, Teague presumed that her daughter would intuit the four directions (east, north, west, and south) and the elements (air, earth, water, and fire) that correspond to them. She discovered that while her daughter did begin by equating north with the earth, she did not correctly identify the elements that correspond to the other three directions. Although initially the mother was disappointed, she came to see that it was more important to permit her child to enjoy working in a magical circle than to ensure that she did it in the *correct* way. Instead of telling the child what to do, Teague waited to be asked before instructing her daughter. Since the child was uncertain of the procedures, she frequently turned to her mother for help and was gently guided in the art of casting a circle. Teague wrote about this incident as a primer for other parents on techniques they could use to foster their children's self-development.

Another parent, Jaq Hawkins, also wants his children to freely choose their own spiritual paths, yet he modifies that wish by asserting, "I've asked myself what I would do if my child fell in with the 'wrong' crowd at the delicate age of fifteen and joined a cult of Jesus freaks. It's a frightening thought, and one I have no answer for as yet" (1994:2). Although parents may hope that their path is followed by their children, most Neo-Pagan parents are willing, at least in principle, to accept that their children will grow to adulthood and choose either another religion or secularism. O'Gaea, author of *The Family Wicca Book,* (1993:24) discloses, "I fantasize that Explorer [her son] will marry a nice Wiccan girl and raise bouncing Wiccan babies—but he might not" (1993:24).

Parents also worry about involving their children in a nontraditional religion. Sue Curewitz, one of the leaders of EarthSpirit Community, was surprised when she learned from a group of teenagers that their parents, who had been active within the Neo-Pagan community, had chosen not to raise their children as Pagans. She believes the parents were afraid their children would suffer repercussions in school or in the larger society if it were known that they were Witches or Neo-Pagans (Curewitz 1989:26). One respondent to "The Pagan Census" stated, "I'd like to raise my son in the craft . . . but I don't want the town bullies to crap on my son for being different" (H. Berger and A. Arthen, n.d.:2433). Jenet, the editor of *The Labryinth,* which describes itself as a newsletter for Pagan families, reiterates this concern by suggesting that parents should be careful using the word *Witch,* or speaking of gods and goddesses, particularly if they live in the Bible Belt or in areas with many fundamentalist Christians. She worries that children, in describing their religious beliefs, will endanger the family in hostile communities (Jenet 1994d:9). However, even if children are not consciously raised in this new religion, they will be influenced by their parents' beliefs and practices. As Ashleen O'Gaea maintains, "Unless you never speak to your kids and never do anything religiously different from your Christian family or neighbors, unless Wicca has not changed your life at all, you are raising your children to the craft" (1993:39).

More pertinent than either parents' ambivalence about giving their children complete freedom or their fear of involving them in their unorthodox lifestyle is the issue of how children are forcing this religion to confront its own process of maturation. As Ceisiwr Serith (1994:ix) contends: "As the young Pagan movement starts to leave its adolescent years behind and its members raise children, the problem becomes more acute. Are we to remain a religion of converts: or will we be able to develop an organic form of Paganism for our children?" Creating an *organic form* of Neo-Paganism will result in a less individualized religion that can be taught to and includes children. It will also increase the probability of the religion's continuing to exist. Religions such as the Shakers declined, at least in part, because they were completely dependent on converts (Kephart 1982). The inclusion of children in new religions transforms the organization and practices of the group (Balch 1988; J. Richardson 1985). With the birth of "Witchlings," as the Witches jokingly call their own children, this new religion could become firmly entrenched in the United States, albeit in an altered form.

Teaching the religion to children involves creating traditions. As Jenet asserts, "In order to leave a Pagan legacy for our children, we need traditions to pass on. In order to have meaningful traditions we will have to make them ourselves" (1995b:14). The creation of traditions is part of the process of routinization. Because children enjoy repetition, the rituals are likely to become systematized. I have already seen elements of this as groups that at one time created new rituals for every Sabbat have begun to repeat the rituals. One Witch justified the reuse of old rituals: "They become more magically powerful with repetition." They also become less spontaneous and less unique.

CHILDREN AND RITUALS

Wicca is an experiential religion that focuses on ritual participation. Because few children have been involved in the movement until recently, both rituals and training have been formulated for adults. Neo-Pagan adults have been trained in ritual practices as well as a variety of skills—such as raising energy, astral projection, performing magic, and using medicinal herbs—through classes, workshops, books, and magazines. Adult Witches read widely about Wicca, Neo-Paganism, and ancient and contemporary

Pagan cultures. Teaching children about Paganism requires a different form of training than that used for adults. Jenet cautions against subjecting children to "Paganism 101 at a lower reading level" (1994c:13).[3] Two journals for Neo-Pagan children are being published, *How About Magic (HAM)* and *Witches and Witchlings*.[4] There are also a growing number of children's books with Neo-Pagan themes. Parents purchase these books and journals to help their children understand elements of Neo-Pagan practice and also feel part of a community. The readings, however, are secondary to involving children in ritual practice.

Neo-Pagan rituals appear welcoming to children, who can actively participate instead of being required to sit still and listen to a sermon. Children are believed to more easily access the divine, as they have not yet fully developed a rational, talking self. But as one Neo-Pagan noted: "How much more do we forget the needs of children attending our magickal rites? More often than not, if they are not shuttled off to a different room to be supervised by the unfortunate of the month, they shuffle and murmur their way through the mechanics of a ceremony in which they have little interest or understanding" (Manor 1994:15). Rituals, which are designed to access the younger self, are created for adults, capable of concentrating on guided meditation and understanding dialogue phrased partially in Elizabethan English.

Children can also break the concentration of the adults. I recently attended an initiation ritual for two women into MoonTide coven, whose members have three children under the age of two.[5] Gordon, a large and active eight-month-old, was in attendance with his mother, as was the youngest child, Lisa, who had turned one month old that day. Lisa's mother, Abby, was the high priestess for the ritual. As the ritual began, Abby gave Lisa to her father, who put her in a carrier, which he hung around his chest. Throughout the ritual Abby became distracted as her baby cried. As soon as the essential part of the ritual was completed, she reached for her newborn and began breastfeeding. Gordon, in the meantime, was being passed from woman to woman to stop him from reaching for the candles on the altar. The moment the ritual ended, the candles were blown out and then moved to prevent Gordon from hurting himself. This coven is committed to creating a family-oriented religion, in which the participation of children is welcomed. However, other groups, particularly those in which only one couple or member has a child, are less tolerant of the distraction of children.

Ceisiwr Serith, a strong advocate of the integration of children into the religion, suggests that they not be included in rituals geared for adults.

"A mistake often made by Pagan parents is to bring the children into Wiccan rituals or, at the least, to compose rituals based closely on what is done by a coven. This arises from a misunderstanding of the role of Mystery Religions in culture" (Serith 1994:8). According to Serith, covens are the modern equivalent of a mystery religion. He contends that in traditional pagan societies mystery groups were always reserved for adults because children not only would disrupt rituals, but also would not benefit from them. He asserts that in these societies children would be included in some community rituals and all family rituals. Serith argues that Neo-Pagans should similarly integrate their children into the religion through both family rituals and daily life practices.

Within Wicca all adult initiates are trained to be priests and priestesses who can create and ultimately lead a ritual. The goal for young children is different; parents want their children to become comfortable with rituals and with basic principles of Paganism. As Northage-Orr (1994) contends, "A love of, and affinity for ritual, like the ability to read, is best cultivated early on" (6).

In family celebrations children are often invited to cast the circle or invoke one of the directions. If the child is old enough, she or he is solicited to read a part of the ritual. The rituals created with the inclusion of children in mind are shorter and worded in language that children can read or at least easily understand. Music, dance, and pageantry, elements that appear in all Neo-Pagan rituals, are easily adapted for children. Children's rituals are less formal than those for adults only, but to help develop a sense of tradition they are more consistent.

Children are taught to put their lives in tune with the cycle of the year through the celebration of the sabbats. Many of these Neo-Pagan celebrations correspond to Christian or secular holidays. As Neo-Pagans frequently note, this is not an accident; many Christian celebrations were devised to coincide with older pagan holidays. For instance, Christmas and Easter fall close to the more ancient celebrations of Yule and the spring equinox respectively. Bringing evergreens into one's home in the middle of the winter, a German pre-Christian practice, is common in Christian countries. Spring fertility symbols of chicks, eggs, and rabbits have been incorporated into the celebration of Easter. Similarly, the integration of some pagan celebrations, such as dancing around the maypole for Beltane (May 1), have been absorbed into popular culture. These convergences help to facilitate the normalization of some Neo-Pagan practices. However, many of the basic differences between Neo-Paganism and more mainstream American religions have also become evident.

In describing his daughter's response to death, Jaq Hawkins notes: "She now accepts reincarnation so naturally that the recent death of one of her human playmates in a house fire was accepted as stoically as such news would be accepted by a Buddhist monk. Her only regret was that she wouldn't see him again in this life, because he would come back as a baby in a different family and not live near her anymore" (Hawkins 1994:2). Neo-Pagans view death as part of the cycle of life. Most Neo-Pagans believe in reincarnation—death is seen as both necessary for renewal and a period of rest. The notion of death as a time of renewal is presented in Deirdre Pulgram Arthen's book for children, *Walking with Mother Earth*. In this simple tale, Mother Earth is met by Lord Death, who is portrayed as a handsome and kindly man. He convinces Mother Earth that she needs a rest. But Mother Earth asks: "'What of my children if I go with you? they cannot survive without my love. I cannot destroy them.' The Lord of Death replied, 'They will not be destroyed. When you leave, their spirits will go deep within to rest as well. When you return, so too will they, refreshed with new life'" (D. Arthen 1992:25).

Death is celebrated at the Sabbat of Samhain (Halloween). Because of the emphasis on rebirth and renewal the holiday is not morbid. It provides an avenue for children to mourn pets, relatives, and friends who have died. Although this holiday shares elements with the Halloween celebrations common in the United States on October 31, its focus is different. Neo-Pagan children make jack-o'-lanterns, dress up in costumes, and go trick-or-treating. However, they also participate in family rituals related to death and mourning.

To involve children in the sabbats, parents engage offspring in activities that evoke the spirit of the season and the upcoming holiday. The activities recommended for Neo-Pagan children are similar to arts and crafts projects that all children do, with this difference: for Neo-Pagans, these projects are devised to help align children with nature and to make them aware of the spiritual significance of the season. For example, at Imbolc (February 1), which celebrates the growing strength of the sun and the approach of spring, parents may teach their children to make candles that can be used in ritual (McArthur 1994). Imbolc is celebrated by lighting a large number of candles to symbolize the increase in the amount of sunlight each day. One Wiccan mother told me that, instead of a formal Imbolc ritual, she and her husband participate in an informal celebration of the holiday with their children. The electric lights are turned off, the house is illuminated with candles, and the parents tell their children stories, such as the myth of the quickening of the sun king in the great mother. The children in turn are invited to tell stories and to reflect on the ending of winter and coming of spring. Making candles is part of the fun and the symbolism of the holiday for the children.

RITES OF PASSAGE

Rites of passage, such as the wiccaning described in the prologue to this book and ceremonies marking the transition from childhood to adulthood, are being created by Neo-Pagans. The welcoming rite—referred to as a wiccaning, a saining, or a paganing—serves a threefold purpose: to introduce the child to the deities and ask for their help and protection as the child grows; to give the community an opportunity to meet and bless the child; and to bring the child into his or her first sacred circle. Welcoming rituals do not commit the child to Pagan goddesses and gods or to a particular spiritual path. At Alex's wiccaning in September 1996 the high priest of his parents' coven addressed the three-month-old: "I, as High Priest can open the [spiritual] door for you. But neither I, nor your parents, nor anyone else can make you walk through that door. When you grow older you must decide whether you will enter this door or choose another—but remember, all walk in spirit and whatever path you pick must therefore be with spirit."[6] As is usual with families in Wicca, the parents are ambivalent about the child's ultimately leaving the religion.

The most varied of the Wiccan rituals that I have attended are sainings. In all instances the child is introduced to the four directions, given good wishes and words of wisdom by the participants, and awarded goddess parents.[7] Other aspects of the ritual, however, vary widely. The wiccaning described in the prologue is the only birth ritual I have attended in which the child's birth blood was used, although I have read about others (Curewitz 1990; Campanelli 1994; McArthur 1994). Other welcoming rituals I have attended have taken place in either the parents' or the high priestess's home, where the use of blood may have been deemed inappropriate. For instance, Alex's parents did not use his birth blood or placenta in his wiccaning, which took place in their dining room, but they do have his placenta in their freezer and plan to bury it in a private ritual before the first frost. Some parents may not be allowed to appropriate the afterbirth at the hospital or birthing center. And some covens or parents may be uncomfortable handling the afterbirth.

MoonTide coven's saining ritual for Lisa anticipated her next rite of passage. All the participants were asked to write words of wisdom on a card that was collected during the ritual by Abby, who promised to keep them unread until Lisa reached puberty. By creating rituals to celebrate their children's sexual maturity, Neo-Pagans hope to address a lack that they feel exists in American culture. As Jenet asserts, "When there is no longer a common extracurricular rite of passage for early adolescents, less savory common experiences have an open field for entry. Parents can hope that today's students have decided not to join in popular culture's rite of passage in gangs, drugs or guns" (1994a:3). Because of the long period that offspring remain dependent in contemporary society, some Neo-Pagans are developing two separate rituals to denote different stages of maturity. The first ritual occurs around the time of puberty and the second when the child graduates from high school or is preparing to leave home. These rituals mark the transition from childhood to adolescence or adulthood for both the parents and their progeny.

Puberty rites are gender specific, unisex rituals. As Serith asserts: "Only a man can make a man, and only a woman can acknowledge a woman" (1994:10). The distinction between the acknowledgment of womanhood and the "making" of manhood is reflected in the puberty rites of Neo-Pagans. Probably more than any others, these rituals highlight the essentialism of gender roles, even though in a latent form, within Wicca.

The girl's ritual underscores her metamorphosis into womanhood. In one rendition of this ritual, a woman who represents the east, the element of air and of intellect, says to the young woman:

Know that as a woman
Once in the month when your blood flows
Or the Moon is full, your mind will be
Open and receptive to things unseen.
Learn to see with the mind's eye,
And listen to the wind
Heed your inner voice,
To be a woman is to gain Wisdom. (Campanelli 1994:43)

The rituals for boys, like those for girls, focus on the spiritual as well as physical changes the boy experiences.[8] Boys are expected to endure an ordeal prior to being recognized as men. The notion of men's proving themselves through an ordeal is common among indigenous groups. Although symbolically Wiccan boys are expected to face their mortality, in reality they are never placed in any danger.

The lack of real risk may mitigate against the boys' experiencing a psychological transformation into manhood. Zack, the founder of HAM, comments about his puberty rite: "I felt that the rite of passage let me into the men's circle and the whole male aspect of magic. But I never really felt I was a man until the truck fell on me. My rite of passage didn't do that" (quoted in Judith 1993:85). The experience that Zack felt resulted in his passage to manhood was one in which he almost died.

Similarly, the girls' rites of passage may or may not result in their feeling like women. The rituals do celebrate and affirm the changes that are occurring in their bodies. However, within the larger society there is little validation of the new status of either females or males. The children remain in middle school, economically dependent on their parents and socially unprepared to begin a family. Furthermore, the dispersion of Neo-Pagans throughout the country means there is no stable face-to-face community to acknowledge the new adult on a daily basis and ensure that the parents change their behavior toward their minor offspring.

These rites of passage nonetheless remain important, as they help to create a community of interest, as discussed in chapter 4. Even if the rituals do not ultimately help to define a passage from youth to adulthood, they provide a shared set of rites in which Wiccan children participate. The inclusion in the sacred circles of extended kin and friends—many from outside Wicca—to celebrate the family's life passages also affirms Wiccans in their practices.

SEX AND THE PAGAN CHILD

What constitutes a healthy notion of sexuality for children and youth in our society is being questioned in parents' magazines, schools, and at times the law courts. As heirs to the counterculture, the Neo-Pagan community is on the whole sexually permissive—accepting open sexuality, homosexuality, bisexuality, and nontraditional family forms, such as group marriages and open marriages. Witches exalt both homosexuality and heterosexuality as magical acts.

The counterculture itself was a harbinger of changes that have become widespread, although not universal, in U.S. society. The sexual revolution, one element of the counterculture, has resulted in the growing acceptance, within many segments of American society, of heterosexual cohabitation, homosexual relationships, and a variety of sexual practices, such as oral sex.[9] The feminist movement, which developed simultaneously with the counterculture, fought for the recognition of women as sexual agents rather than objects and the elimination of the dichotomy between nonsexual, "decent" women (*good girls*) and sexually active, "loose" women (*bad girls*). In late modernity sexuality and sexual expression have become one element of life choices (Giddens 1992).

The sexual revolution has expanded to youths, who are in increasing numbers participating in their first coitus in early adolescence. Rubin (1990) notes that young people no longer define a committed relationship as one that they believe will last forever. The relationship may last several months or a year, but there is no expectation that it will last a lifetime. Love, heretofore viewed as the basis of a committed relationship, is seen as fleeting. According to Rubin, the change in sexual attitude is greater for girls than for boys, although both are affected. Rubin contends that the attitude toward sex of American youth can be summed up in two words, entitlement and tolerance.

The celebration of sexuality within Wicca has resonance in the larger society in late modernity. Nonetheless, Neo-Pagan parents are concerned that their children be neither pressured into premature sexuality nor taken away from them by social agencies that view their attitude toward sex as too radical. At the same time, these parents maintain the importance of presenting sex to their children in a positive light. This ambivalence is expressed in a growing uneasiness among Neo-Pagan parents about the actual expression of sexuality in rituals and at festivals. As Jenet notes: "Now that I am a parent, the traditional Beltane games that are frequently of a playful sexual context make me a bit nervous. . . . Sexuality is a powerful tool, an emblem of the union that sparked the Universe, and as a tool it can be misused, abused and neglected, but well used it brings joy to our lives. . . . It is an enormous challenge to teach our children a healthy view of sexuality" (Jenet 1994b:4).

Rituals, particularly those that occur in the spring at either the equinox or Beltane, have a sexual flavor, because fertility is being celebrated. At Beltane the goddess and god are invoked in their roles as consorts. The rituals focus on fertility in nature and among people. The symbolic expression of sexuality can be quite explicit. At one Beltane ritual I attended, at which no children were present, men and women formed into two winding circles facing one another. People whirled by one another, kissing or attempting to kiss the new person who faced them. The atmosphere was charged. At one point everyone in the room took off their robes and stood sweaty and naked in the makeshift temple of the high priest and priestess's home. At another Beltane ritual, attended by two children about five and eight years old, there was no nudity. However, again there was a sexually charged atmosphere during the ritual. The man invoking the green man, or male aspect, was dressed in a short green robe open at the sides, so that as he moved his underpants were revealed. He went around the circle kissing all the women and challenging the men in the group. It was a playful moment, with women moving away and mocking being chased, or complaining that the green man had bad aim when he kissed. He was carrying a staff and jokingly challenged the other men in the circle to compare the size of their staffs with his. He then joined the priestess, who was invoking the goddess in the center of the circle, in a dance that implied a sexual union. In mundane life the green man and the priestess were soon to be married, and their dance was clearly lustful. However, as they both remained dressed, the dance was only symbolic of the sexual union.

Nudity at rituals, sunbathing, or dancing around a open fire at night are accepted behaviors at festivals. There is both an awareness and concern within the community about the transmission of AIDS. At one festival, multicolored condoms were made available throughout the campsite for anyone who might want one. Many of the children availed themselves of the condoms, blowing them up to use as balloons or filling them with water to throw at one another.

Neo-Pagan parents, most of whom have participated in the campsite dances and open sexuality, are reevaluating the appropriateness of that environment for their children. A forty-year-old woman expressed her concern that her fourteen-year-old daughter might be "hit-up" at a festival they were about to attend. The child had reached puberty, and though still a minor, she looked like a woman. As more Neo-Pagan children reach puberty, more adults are concerned about protecting them from unsolicited sexual advances.

There was an outcry within the Neo-Pagan community against Gavin and Yvonne Frost, who, in their book *The Witch's Bible,* recommended the use of sex in initiatory rituals and rites of passage to adulthood for boys and girls. The Covenant of the Goddess (CoG) went on record as condemning the practice.[10] The book and the protest against it by prominent individuals of the Wiccan community publicly raised the issue of potential sexual abuse within covens in general and particularly against adolescent girls. As one high priest wrote, "For a Priest to even suggest sexual involvement with a junior convener, student, or anyone else who comes to him for spiritual guidance is coercive. It exploits a condition of 'power over' and amounts to sexual abuse" (James 1994:15). Similarly, a high priestess of another coven contended:

> Unscrupulous egocentric men in our present culture use any means possible to take advantage of women sexually. . . . Since the men who continue in these practices, aided by the complacency of the women around them, obviously will not give up their "power over" willingly, let me address the women. It is up

to us to protect each other. The practices of sexual initiatory rites and coercion (especially with minors) is not at all right. It is unhealthy and harmful to our sisters, not to mention against the law, and it should be stopped now. (Athene 1994:16)

The issue of sexual exploitation within the coven, particularly of minors, is fourfold. First, as participants in a feminist form of spirituality Wiccans are concerned that exploitation and the misuse of power not develop. On the one hand, open sexuality within Wicca has been seen as liberating to women—eradicating the good girl/bad girl dichotomy of the double standard while recognizing women's sexuality. On the other hand, there is concern that women not become the objects of sexual exploitation, particularly young women who are the most vulnerable. Second, members of the Neo-Pagan community have been working toward having their religious practices viewed as legitimate by the larger society. News stories of sexual abuse by Witches stymie such efforts. Third, any hint of sexual exploitation could negatively affect Wiccans in child custody cases. Fourth, although some members may be exploitative, the community as a whole wants to protect its children, as the protests against the Frosts revealed. In response to the negative reactions to their book, the Frosts eliminated the most inflammatory passages from its next edition.

Neo-Pagans are attempting to define what is a healthy sexual atmosphere for children. In "Youth and Maiden Lovemaking," which appeared in *HAM* in 1990, Zack Darling-Ferns, who was then fourteen years old, presented his view of responsible sex for Pagan youth. He began the article, "A lot to being Pagan is being a good lover. My attitude is, why not start sooner [rather] than later?" (Darling-Ferns 1990:10). Zack advocates that youth learn to practice responsible sex, which he describes as having four aspects: one, the practice of safe sex, through the use of either condoms or "outercourse"; two, the use of birth control to avoid unwanted pregnancies; three, sex occurring only between two consenting parties; and four, both partners' respecting the other's privacy by keeping the details of their sexual encounter between themselves. Since Zack was writing as a youth to other young people, he cautioned that would-be lovers consider parental approval or disapproval before embarking on a romantic union. He noted that most Neo-Pagan parents are supportive of their adolescent children's sexuality, but that some parents—especially non-Pagans—may be more conservative.

Zack's article was controversial among Neo-Pagan adults. Some Neo-Pagan adults were apprehensive that the article might give the impression that minors were being encouraged by the community to have sex (Judith

1993:83). The issue of children and sex is a difficult one for Neo-Pagans. When the religion involved primarily adults, dealing with sexuality was relatively easy. Consenting adults are legally free to revel in their sexuality. The potential for problems to arise was always there, but they were problems among adults.

The appropriateness of sexual behavior, however, is an issue that is magnified when children are involved. Pagan parents fear that courts or child protection agencies may remove children from their homes because of Neo-Pagan sexual practices or open nudity. Custody hearings or decisions about foster children make this anxiety particularly acute. Anne, a tall lithe woman with two lively children, is fighting her former husband to maintain custody of their son and daughter. She has had to defend her religious practice as well as the open sexuality within the religion. Her husband was a Witch, who left the religion shortly after ending the marriage. His legal brief for custody of the children accused Anne of corrupting his minor children by providing them with Pagan coloring books that depicted nude goddesses. Anne has been required to show in court that her religious practices will not harm her children. She has been enjoined by the court from including her children in Wiccan rituals.

Most parents do not want their children pushed into premature sexuality. Like many liberal parents, Neo-Pagans confront the problem of defining when their children are adults. Judith (1993), in her interview of three adolescents who were raised as Neo-Pagans, found that both of the young women she spoke to felt social pressure within the community to become sexually active, although they also claimed that their communities' sexual openness had given them a healthier attitude toward sex than their peers.

As more Neo-Pagan youth reach puberty, the controversy about sexuality will become more acute. The notion of sex as both beautiful and magical is so embedded in rituals and in the attitudes of a large segment of the community that I suspect it will remain. However, as more children begin to mature within the Wiccan community, rituals and festivals may have fewer instances of open sexuality. The tone of the festivals has to some degree already become quieter. Although young adults may enjoy drumming and dancing through the night, young parents are anxious that the campsites be quiet enough for their children and themselves to sleep.

MAGICAL CHILDREN

Neo-Pagan children are taught to view the world through the magical and mystical lenses. As Ashleen O'Gaea contends, "Nearly everything we do at home can be done with Wicca in mind. From rearranging a room to brushing hair, everything can be a spell. . . . And if we share mundane blessings with our children it will become second nature to them" (1993:25). Within Wicca, all of life and its activities become imbued with spirituality. Joan, who had been raised in a Wiccan family and was pregnant with her first child when I interviewed her, noted that although the child would grow up knowing about all religions and would have the option of choosing a religion, the child would be raised "understanding the healing aspect and communicating with the animals and nature and taking on the [magical] responsibility—the child will be raised with that every day of its life and that will be very natural; and the child will know that is from the craft" (Joan Interview 1989).

Susan, the high priestess of the MoonTide coven, is starting a nursery school for Pagan children that she hopes to expand into a day school. She told me that the goddess had guided her in this decision. Initially, she had not wanted to become involved with educating young children, having already raised a family of her own; but "the goddess hit me on the side of the head with the proverbial two-by-four and I knew this was something I had to do." She came to believe the creation of a school was necessary to protect Neo-Pagan children from becoming psychically and magically crippled.

Susan contends that she and other Neo-Pagan adults were harmed as children in "nominally" secular schools. Imps, spirit guides, and god forces that the child spoke to were reinterpreted in the schools as imaginary friends. Susan argues that we were all trained to ignore and reinterpret psychic experiences as either coincidences, imagination, or psychological displacement. She asserts that Pagan adults must now spend their time and energy trying to revitalize their psychic and magical abilities, which they were naturally attuned to as children. Susan feels that the next generation must be saved from being thwarted as their parents have been.

According to Susan, the public schools, which claim to be secular, actually incorporate Judeo-Christian ideals and celebrations. For example, children make Christmas cards and sing Christmas carols in school. Halloween is a time to decorate the classroom with pictures of disfigured women, who are referred to as witches, dressed in black, and flying on broomsticks. Susan feels that, on the whole, public schools are harmful to Neo-Pagan children. Every Neo-Pagan parent to whom I have spoken has expressed similar sentiments. One Pagan on the Internet notes, "I didn't like seeing my stepdaughter coming home parroting the cowan [secular], no blatantly Xian [Christian] . . . stuff she was exposed to at school. . . . Think what our childhoods might have been like if we'd been brought up by people that didn't force us to disbelieve the guidance of the spirits" (Magical Rat 1994).

Although children are believed to be born in synchrony with the spiritual world, their natural ability can be either developed or impeded. Parents use a number of techniques to help their children develop their magical abilities, including meditation, rituals, and other forms of raising energy. To overcome the larger society's skepticism about magic, parents use concrete examples to demonstrate to their children that magic does work. For instance, O'Gaea (1993) points out to her son his successful use of his psychic powers when he was thinking or talking about a friend and that person then telephoned.

Some aspects of the mystical and magical beliefs and practices of Neo-Pagans have resonance in more mainstream religions. Catholics light candles to ask saints to intercede on their behalf. Fundamentalist Christians speak of Christ's guiding them or being part of their everyday life. However, even with these similarities there remains a fundamental difference between espousing Witchcraft and participating in Christianity. Danzger (1989) notes that being a Christian, even a fundamentalist or a devout one, is a form of "hyperconformism" in the United States. In comparison, Witchcraft and magic are treated with either disdain or fear. Although the disdain and fear of magical practices affect all Neo-Pagans, these attitudes especially complicate for parents the involvement of their children in Wiccan practices.

Because Neo-Pagans live in the secular world, their children are required to bifurcate their lives into the magical, enchanted world of Wicca and the secular society. Most Neo-Pagan adults compartmentalize their lives successfully. Magic and mysticism do not become directly or openly incorporated into their professional or mundane lives. Many remain in the "broom closet" in the larger society. Even those who are open about their religion do not normally conduct rituals or enter trances at work. Children, particularly younger children, who are trained to participate in meditation and working magic may have a more difficult time compartmentalizing. Jenet contends that "As parents who are Pagan and Wiccan we need to teach our children a series of 'know-hows' in order to know how to live in two worlds" (1995a:10). Eluba, the mother of two Pagan children, similarly notes, "if you have them [children] in normal schools they have to lead a double life." However, she goes on to suggest that, while this creates some difficulty for the children, "the skills that being part of a Pagan community are imparting to them will be invaluable to them as they grow up—when they are grown up—they will be nourished and encouraged" (Eluba Interview 1990).

In an interview before her first pregnancy, the mother of the boy whose wiccaning I described in the prologue, now a mother of two Neo-Pagan children, defined Paganism as "the [celebration of the] cycle of the seasons and the full moon rituals and working with symbol and ritual and those sorts of things—and it is wonderful" (Jane Interview 1987). Neo-Pagan children are born into a community that celebrates nature, through both rituals and ecological practices. The children are encouraged to recycle, create gardens, and pick up trash.

Many aspects of Neo-Pagan children's upbringing are the same as that of other middle-class children in the United States. Neo-Pagan parents try to teach their children self-respect, respect for others, and respect for the ecosystem. However, Neo-Pagan children are also encouraged by both their parents and the Neo-Pagan community to develop their magical personas and psychic abilities, through rituals and other mystical practices.

Almost every Witch I have spoken to has raised concerns about the negative stereotypes that surround the term *Witch*. This is intensified for children. Joan, an adult raised in a Wiccan family, remarks about her childhood: "Kids at that age—still in grammar school, are nasty anyway, looking for someone to be the scapegoat, like the fat kid or the one with braces and for us it was the Witches" (Joan Interview 1989). A generation later, things have not changed significantly. Eluba notes, "In some ways it's been incredibly difficult for them [her children]. Children are nothing if not little animals of peer pressure and being different is difficult no matter who you are" (Eluba Interview 1990). Because they worry that their children may suffer discrimination, parents, more than other participants, are eager for their religious practice be seen as legitimate. The growth in the number of children being born to adherents is forcing a decentralized community to start to rethink and redefine itself. Witchcraft and Neo-Paganism, which grew out of the counterculture, are becoming more conservative. Tradition, continuity, and restrained sexuality become more important as children enter the circle.

CHAPTER 6

The Routinization of Creativity

She [the Goddess] Changes Everything She Touches and
Everything She Touches Changes.

These are the words of a Neo-Pagan chant that is most frequently
heard at spring rituals. Changes—in the self, in nature, and in the social
world—are all celebrated within Neo-Paganism.[1] However, as the religion itself changes from a fluid structure emphasizing individual innovation
and creativity to a more formalized religion, there is a growing schism
between those who support or work for structural modification of the
religion and those who oppose these changes.

Wicca gives the impression of being antithetical to routinization
because of the fluidity of coven membership and the lack of a uniform
dogma. The development of rituals by covens are creative acts, involving
dance, music, art, and poetry. Each coven's rituals take on their own flavor—involving different chants and particular words used in casting the
circle or calling in the directions. However, groups are becoming more
alike as chants, incantations, and ideas for rituals, such as wiccanings, are
shared. The change, which is neither unidirectional nor without opposi-
tion, is occurring through three avenues: the sharing of information about
rituals, chants, and magical practices on the communication networks;
the increased influence of well-known Witches; and the creation of large-
scale Neo-Pagan organizations, Neo-Pagan churches, and the Unitarian
Universalist Association Neo-Pagan group, Covenant of the Unitarian
Universalist Pagans (CUUPs).

ROUTINIZATION

In his classic work on routinization of religions, Weber contends,
"Prophets and priests are the twin bearers of the systematization and rationalization of religious ethics" (Weber 1964:45). According to Weber,

religions are their most fluid and innovative during the charismatic period, during which prophets are able to reinterpret traditional religious injunctions and practices or create new ones because of their perceived personal power. This period is short-lived, however, as after the death of the prophet the religion either disintegrates or becomes codified by the charismatic leader's disciples. In their efforts to maintain the prophet's insights, the disciples reify his or her teachings and aid in the formation of a new priest class that interprets those teachings. Ironically, it is the attempt by the disciples to capture the prophet's charisma that results in the development of routinization.

Weber argues that, although magical practitioners may form into guilds, they are immune to routinization because they do not develop a congregation of worship. He views magicians as manipulators of demons, not as worshippers of deities (Weber 1964:47). Although today's Neo-Pagans and Witches are magical practitioners, they are also members of a religion that forms groups to worship.

Within Wicca there are celebrity Witches. These are individuals who have written books that are widely read within the community—for example, Margot Adler, Starhawk, and Scott Cunningham—or have established a Neo-Pagan network, organized festivals, or published newsletters and journals—for example, Selena Fox of Circle Sanctuary in Wisconsin and Andras and Deirdre Arthen of the EarthSpirit Community in Massachusetts.[2] These individuals share some characteristics with Weber's description of charismatic leaders: they are viewed as magically powerful individuals who are influential throughout the Witchcraft community. However, the social context in which charismatic leaders and their devotees develop has altered drastically since the period in which Weber wrote. Beckford argues that the growth of mass media, public relations, image management, commercialism, pluralism of religious beliefs, and relativism has made Weber's model of charismatic authority no longer applicable to religions of late modernity (1992a:167–68). Most importantly, it is the skepticism towards authority, organizational hierarchy, and leadership in late modernity that mitigates against the formation within Wicca of charismatic leaders in the Weberian sense.

Although the routinization of Wicca has similarities to Weber's description of the routinization of charisma, it is different in three main ways. First, much of the routinization of Wicca has occurred through the sharing of information in books and journals and on the Internet rather than through the systematization of charisma by disciples. Second, the individuals who are attempting to form churches or umbrella organizations justify their leadership based on their administrative skills, not their religious purity. Third, it is not the magical qualities of charisma that are being routinized but the spontaneity and creativity of religious expression.

The model that best frames the process of routinization occurring in this new religious movement comes from organizational theory. In "The Iron Cage Revisited," DiMaggio and Powell (1983) argue that the Weberian model of routinization is no longer applicable to the present business environment, as the homogenization of businesses is not the result of increased efficiency. Instead, they propose three alternative mechanisms for homogenization: coercive, mimetic, and normative isomorphism. Organizations experience coercive isomorphism by responding to pressure from other organizations on which they depend or from government regulations. Mimetic isomorphism develops because of the organization's uncertainty about its technologies, goals, or solutions. Organizations, therefore, follow the lead of others that appear to be successful. Normative isomorphism is the result of professionalization, which through the educational process, professional organizations, and networks helps to create and spread similarities among organizations.

Dimaggio and Powell maintain that the growth of homogenization—within both the business community that they examined and other spheres as diverse as medicine and college textbook publication—emerges from structuration of late modernity as described by Giddens (Dimaggio and Powell 1983:147). According to Dimaggio and Powell, structuration consists of four parts: "An increase in the extent of interactions among organizations in the field; the emergence of sharply defined interorganizational structures of domination and patterns of coalition; an increase in the information load with which organizations in a field must contend; and the development of a mutual awareness among participants in a set of organizations that they are involved in a common enterprise" (1983:148). All of these factors, except a "sharply defined interorganizational structure of domination," are developing within Neo-Paganism. Although routinization of the religion is, in part, the outgrowth of the aging of its participants, the form of this routinization is consistent with the growth of homogeneity in other organizational spheres of late modernity.

Dimaggio and Powell believe the development of this new form of rationalization in business organizations results from increased government regulation and professionalization, both of which lead to similarities developing among businesses, even when those similarities are neither profitable nor rational. Coercive, mimetic, and normative isomorphism are involved to varying degrees in the changes I have witnessed within Wicca. Some aspects of mimetic isomorphism have existed in Neo-Paganism and Witchcraft since the religion's origins. People formed covens after reading influential books, such as *Drawing Down the Moon* (Adler 1979) and *The Spiral Dance* (Starhawk 1979), or after attending a workshop or set of classes on Witchcraft. However, initially covens were quite innovative in their interpretation and integration of Neo-Pagan and Witchcraft materials.

Standardization, nonetheless, has been increasing. The uncertainty of dealing with the problems that arise in creating a new religion combined with the need for legitimacy results in the development of isomorphism. Mimetic isomorphism occurs when specific chants, artwork, or other aspects of rituals spread among individual practitioners or groups. Festivals are an important avenue for the dissemination of information about practices among the adherents of this new religion. Chants and songs are frequently collected and distributed over computer networks. For example, nine years ago a collection of fifty songs for Yule was distributed on the Internet. The tunes are well known, often those of Christmas carols, but with substitute words appropriate for the celebration of the Neo-Pagan holiday. Linda made copies of the "songbook" for members of the Circle of Light coven.

The requirements for classification as a legal religious organization with tax-exempt status and the right to perform legally binding marriages are too few and too loose to lead to coercive isomorphism. However, those groups that have obtained legal status are concerned that neither negative publicity nor their own activities result in their losing that status. For Neo-Pagans who are working through CUUPs or who have independently joined the Unitarian Universalists, the internal structure of that organization puts some restraints on their practices. For instance, within the Unitarian Universalist Association (UUA) no group can be exclusionary. CUUPs meetings are therefore open to nonmembers within their local Unitarian Universalist congregation.[3]

Normative isomorphism is the result of growing professionalism. Although Wicca has no one standard training for high priestesses and high priests, a network is attempting to establish standards of practice.[4] These standards remain loose and are at best only partially defined, but the process has begun. Some Neo-Pagans are entering seminaries to be trained. Inanna Arthen, a former member of the inner circle of EarthSpirit Community, is presently in her second year of study for a Masters of Divinity degree at Harvard University Divinity

School. She is the first person accepted to Harvard Divinity School to work toward a degree in Neo-Pagan ministry. Other Neo-Pagans are studying or have studied at Harvard toward a ministry in Unitarian Universalism, and Neo-Pagans have received divinity degrees from other universities as well.

The tension that has existed since the beginning of the religion between spontaneity and homogeneity is giving way to greater routinization. The growth of information networks, the desire for greater legitimacy, the increased number of adherents, and the development of a professional ethic are all pressuring the religion to change. The debates that surrounded Andras and Deirdre Arthen's attempt to become full-time paid employees of EarthSpirit Community (ESC) highlight the desire by some members of the community for change and the problems others foresee in the development of a more structured religious practice. Although ESC failed to raise funds to support its capital development fund or to establish a full-time paid staff, its attempt to become a financially stable organization provides one model for change. The debates go beyond ESC's efforts to become a more financially secure organization and reach the heart of the problems that surround all efforts to create large-scale Neo-Pagan organizations—that is, what sources are available to finance a Neo-Pagan organization? And what effect would these organizations have on the development of hierarchy and individual or coven autonomy?

EARTHSPIRIT COMMUNITY AND ROUTINIZATION

Andras Corban Arthen founded the EarthSpirit Community in the Boston area in the early 1980s. He and his wife Deirdre are the major forces in the organization, which is run by an inner group. At the time of the debates about the creation of a paid clergy members of this inner group all belonged to the same coven, the Athanor Fellowship. As an expression of the closeness of their relationship with one another many of the members of the coven took the last name Arthen, which Andras and Deirdre had created for themselves when they were married. The Athanor Fellowship has dissolved, but the covens that grew out of it remain interconnected, as part of the Glainn Sidhr Order of Witches. This inner group of people is largely responsible for printing the monthly newsletter, arranging open circles for four or five sabbats a year, and organizing several weekend-long festivals each year, all of which are run under ESC auspices. They previously also published a magazine, *FireHeart*.

ESC's relationship to the larger Neo-Pagan community is reminiscent, in some respects, of what Stark and Bainbridge refer to as *client cults*—that is, a core group that provides services to individuals for a fee.[5] Stark and Bainbridge contend that in these groups, clients never become integrated into the organization, although they do repeatedly seek its services. To explicate their meaning, Stark and Bainbridge use the analogy of "the relationship between therapist and patient or between consultant and client" (1985:26). Some members of ESC have only a minimal commitment to the organization.[6] They pay fees when they choose to attend open sabbats and festivals and receive a newsletter that they may or may not read, but otherwise they have little contact with the organization. In other respects, however, ESC differs from Stark and Bainbridge's description of a client cult. Some members of ESC volunteer time to help organize events or prepare mailings, and they attend most if not all of ESC events. Although these individuals are not part of the inner core, they form a second circle of those who are actively involved in the organization. Some people join the inner core after working on ESC projects and becoming involved with the Glainn Sidhr Order of Witches. The inner core is relatively stable. Some people leave because they become disenchanted with the organization or because they move away from the area; others join the group.

Another aspect of ESC that makes it fall outside the definition of a client cult is that it serves to create a community among New England Neo-Pagans. ESC festivals bring together Neo-Pagans from all over the country, and their open sabbats involve people from throughout New England. Furthermore, members of the Glainn Sidhr Order of Witches are integrated into the larger Neo-Pagan community. They attend handfastings, wiccanings, and funerals of other covens' members, and at times participate in their sabbats. Many people have joined the religion after attending one of the open circles or festivals sponsored by ESC.

At the time the debates began in 1990, Andras and Deirdre had been working as full-time administrators of ESC for seven years. During this time the number of activities sponsored by the group increased—there are now twelve retreats a year. Some of these, like Rites of Spring, are seasonal festivals, whereas others are aimed at particular groups—for example, women's or men's mystery circles or circles of recovery for people with addictions. Attendance at festivals, workshops, and circles is open to members and nonmembers alike. ESC has an office in Andras and Deirdre's home. Until the fall of 1996 when they and seven other members of their group moved to western Massachusetts they were located in a Boston suburb. Since giving up their full-time jobs, Andras and Deirdre have supported themselves through Deirdre's small psychotherapy practice, classes on magic and Witchcraft each teaches at the Cambridge Adult Education Center or local occult bookstores, and a salary generated from the proceeds of festivals and open sabbats. When I began attending ESC open events, an admission fee was collected to cover expenses whenever a space was rented for the event. Rituals held in state parks or other open areas were always free. This has recently changed—at the 1996 Beltane ritual participants were asked to donate between $3 and $5 to cover expenses of a ritual held in the park.

Although Andras and Deirdre maintain a very modest lifestyle, I have heard whispers for several years from participants in ESC festivals that the organization has not honestly informed the Neo-Pagan community about the income generated at Rites of Spring and possibly other functions. Although I have no evidence that ESC has misrepresented their earnings there is nonetheless concern about Andras and Deirdre's economic dependence on the work they do for EarthSpirit. This concern has increased as Andras and Deirdre have requested funds to help pay their salaries. They claim that they are not earning enough money to support themselves and their children at an acceptable level. Andras stated in the ESC newsletter, two months before the birth of their second child, that after paying for health insurance and social security he and Deirdre jointly earned $23,000. He estimated that, given their educational backgrounds, ages, and work experience, they could each earn between $30,000 and $50,000 a year with benefits if they took regular jobs (A. Arthen 1991a:3).

ESC was at this time striving to consolidate its economic base, not only by attempting to generate enough money to pay salaries initially to Andras and Deirdre and ultimately to other members of the staff, but also by soliciting money to buy land. The impetus to buy land stemmed from problems surrounding Rites of Spring. As attendance at this festival grew, finding facilities large enough to house or provide campsites for all the participants became more difficult. Rites of Spring usually takes place at a children's summer camp prior to its opening for the season. Problems arose as neighbors complained that they saw Neo-Pagans sunbathing in the nude around the lake. Some camps became unwilling to rent to ESC again. Furthermore, as Andras noted in the ESC newsletter more than $100,000 had been spent in ten years of renting these facilities (A. Arthen 1991b:3). Andras concluded that the Neo-Pagan community under ESC auspices should buy a parcel of land in central Massachusetts. He envisioned this as "a place with enough land, facilities and privacy in which to hold gatherings; where we could sponsor workshops, seminars and intensives; that could support a Pagan based school and summer camp; that would include a Pagan burial ground; that could be used by other Pagan organizations as well as by non-Pagans whose values were congruent with ours" (A. Arthen 1991b:3–4).

The issue of giving money to sustain and expand ESC divided the members. When ESC requested funds, some members sent money and supported the creation of an endowment to provide staff salaries. Others feared that this would result in a paid clergy, the formation of a hierarchy, and a decrease in coven autonomy. The division between those who sent money and those who objected to the creation of the fund cut across the lines of active and inactive members. The debate began with a letter in the October 1990 ESC newsletter, in which Willow, a member of ESC, contended: "ESC is like a large corporation or a church without walls. . . . Unlike other denominations our 'church' has demanded selfless full time service from its spiritual leaders without giving them the benefit of housing, health care or a pension. We seem to expect full time devotion without regard for the real security needs of our ministers and their children born and unborn" (Willow 1990:10).

Willow used the terms *church* and *denomination* interchangeably. In nonacademic milieus the terminology is less rigorously employed, but Willow also wanted to legitimize her religious practice by placing it within the mainstream of churches and denominations. Letters to the ESC newsletter disagreed with her contention that Andras and Deirdre should be supported as clergy by the Neo-Pagan and Witchcraft community. As another participant in the debate suggested, "there is a large percentage of the Community made up of other coven traditions, who attend ESC gatherings and Neo-Pagan social events, but do not see Andras and Deirdre or other members of Athanor as their clergy" (Pigman 1991:16).

The issue of maintaining different traditions is important within the Neo-Pagan community; it is viewed as central to maintaining religious autonomy. Yet the fracturing of religious practice into different traditions is, at least in part, what makes it difficult for Andras and Deirdre to consolidate power based on charismatic leadership. They may be charismatic leaders of the network of covens that are at the center of ESC; however, they are requesting economic support not as religious leaders but as administrators. This model for the creation of a religious bureaucracy is different from that offered by Weber. Andras and other core members of ESC do not emphasize their religious purity or ability to interpret sacred texts, but rather their administrative skills.

Some participants in the debate, such as Bill of MotherChant, a Phila-delphia-based coven, argued that Andras and Deirdre should be supported because of their organizational skills (1991:4–10). But others are concerned about the control that Andras, Deirdre, or the core group of ESC have over the organization. As one participant claims,

> If EarthSpirit Community is primarily a religious organization that plans and provides "worship services" (i.e., rituals) and clergy related services (such as officiating at handfastings etc.),[7] then it is certainly appropriate for Athanor, as guardians of a particular spiritual/religious tradition, to oversee the provision of such services. But if ESC is to become a member-supported nonprofit organization with paid professional staff, then it feels important to me to have the larger community somehow represented. (Swilling 1991:13)

In their study of the political economies of new religious movements, Bird and Westley (1988) concluded that many new religions are unstable because they are economically dependent on volunteerism and on payment for services rather than salaries. Many of the people who have volunteered time to ESC have become burned out. The organization may collapse, and with it many of the festivals that bring Neo-Pagans together. ESC can be viewed as attempting to stabilize its organization through the development of an economic base. However, the concern of many Neo-Pagans is that if it becomes a funded organization ESC will gain too much influence in defining the religious beliefs and practices of the larger Neo-Pagan community. Wallis (1977) in his study of scientology and J. Richardson (1979) in his work on the Jesus movement documented how a core group was able to define the boundaries of belief and practice within their religion by gaining control of the organization.

Because there is no democratic structure or accountability within ESC, many Neo-Pagans fear that ESC may become dictatorial. ESC has a board of directors composed of Neo-Pagans from several different traditions and groups. The board, however, is only advisory; all decisions remain in the hands of Andras, Deirdre, and the small circle of people who run ESC. Although Andras and core members of ESC acknowledge that the organization is not democratic, they claim that they have no desire to gain control over other groups or individuals. Andras asserts that the lack of democratic structure facilitates the completion of ESC projects. The core members of ESC work diligently organizing festivals, running meetings, editing a newsletter, and—until 1996—publishing a magazine; they understandably want to be paid for their work. However, it is politically naive of the leaders to suggest that their being given control over land purchased by the larger Neo-Pagan community would not give them power over other groups.

In an interview I conducted with Inanna Arthen at Harvard Divinity School, she spoke about the issues that surrounded ESC's request for funds. At the time of the debates she was a member of the organization's inner circle.

> A question that was brought up even in that debate in the newsletter was who's going to have access [to the land that was purchased]—and there was never any clear answer to that, as even the people inside EarthSpirit could not make up their minds. [There was a] constant ongoing debate whether this should be a residence or whether it should be a conference center and whether it should be just open to the people living there or should not be open to the public—because that raises all sorts of legal questions and privacy questions. The debates just went on in circles about this because they were really just unanswerable questions at that juncture. (Inanna Arthen Interview 1996)

Access to the facilities was one of the concerns members of the Neo-Pagan community had about giving funding to EarthSpirit Community. Even if the lands were open to the larger Neo-Pagan community, it was feared that ESC would have too much power in determining how the land was used and which groups had access.

Less than $2,000 was collected during the year the debates raged in the newsletter. Some groups who were active members of ESC have left—members of several covens told me they let their ESC membership expire. The break did not stem solely from ESC's attempt to become a funded organization. Some covens boycotted Rites of Spring and ended their ESC membership because they disagreed with Deirdre and Andras's determination about who could exchange work for partial or full payment for admission to the festival. The ruptures that developed for other reasons were exacerbated by ESC's attempt to gain an economic base.

After receiving no substantial economic support from the Neo-Pagan community, ESC cut back on some of their activities—they held fewer open rituals, conducted one less festival a year, and stopped printing *FireHeart*. ESC nonetheless remains an important organization within the Neo-Pagan community. Although ESC was not able to purchase land, in the fall of 1996 some members of the inner group of the organization jointly bought 130 acres in western Massachusetts, on which they are living communally. Other members of the inner group will join the commune after they sell their homes and get their other affairs in order. The group hopes to eventually use the land to hold small gatherings and as a conference center. The larger gatherings organized by ESC, such as Rites of Spring, will still be held at rented sites (A. Arthen 1997).

OTHER ROUTES TO ROUTINIZATION

Circle Sanctuary—commonly called Circle—is an example of a group that has successfully incorporated as a church, bought land, and economically supports clergy. Based in Wisconsin, Circle is the largest Neo-Pagan organization in the United States (Melton 1992:327). Its newsletter, *Circle Network News,* has fifteen thousand subscribers (Kelly 1992:141). Of the several festivals a year the group holds on its land, the largest is Pagan Spirit Gathering. Circle also holds seminars, maintains a Neo-Pagan network, and actively helps Neo-Pagan individuals and groups in the United States and Canada who believe they have suffered from discrimination due to their religious beliefs and practices.

Circle was formed in 1974 by Selena Fox, her romantic partner, Jim Alan, and a small group of people that regularly met at the Fox-Alan household. Four years later they incorporated as a legal church in Wisconsin and began the publication of *Circle Network News.* In 1980 they held their first Pagan Spirit Gathering. The church purchased two hundred acres of land in the foothills near Madison, Wisconsin, in 1983. In 1986 Circle was challenged by local authorities on a zoning ordinance and after a two-year battle won the right to have their land zoned for church use (Guiley 1989:66–67).

Jim Alan left Circle in 1986, two years after his relationship with Selena Fox ended. Selena Fox and the man she married in 1986, Dennis Carpenter, remain central figures in the organization and management of Circle Sanctuary (Guiley 1989:129–30).[8] They and the other members of their group live communally on the church lands.

One of my contacts in the Boston area believes that part of the reason ESC was unable to solicit funds for the creation of a similar enterprise in Massachusetts is because of concerns that grew out of the purchase of land by Circle. According to this person, some individuals within the Neo-Pagan community claim to have contributed funds towards the purchase and development of the land in Wisconsin with the unwritten understanding that they would have open access to the land. They maintain that once the land was purchased, their contributions became defined as donations and the land became the sole property of Circle. I have no proof that these allegations are true. Whether they are or not is less important than that they have made Neo-Pagans wary of contributing money to the purchase of land by a Neo-Pagan organization without a clear and legally binding understanding of what rights the contributors would have to the land.

Although ESC's desire to create a paid bureaucratic/priest class has been stymied, it is still part of the process of routinization. Through its newsletter, magazine, and many festivals, ESC participates in the development of mimetic isomorphism within Neo-Paganism. The Internet, books, journals, and other sources of information are frequently referred to because a new religion involves many uncertainties. People starting covens are confronted with a series of questions and problems, such as how to organize their groups, deal with interpersonal conflicts, and develop rituals. Judy Harrow, a high priestess and former officer of Covenant of the Goddess (CoG), suggested, "we need to look beyond the coven, sometimes, when special expertise is needed. We have many ways to locate our specialists: publications, festivals, organizations like CoG, the various Wiccan traditions and lineages and informal local networks. We can build consultation and referral networks" (Harrow 1991:36). Ms. Harrow is less suggesting new ways for Witches to learn from one another than listing the ways in which Witches already share information. CoG, a loosely organized national federation of covens, is one avenue through which information is spread within the Neo-Pagan community. It has a newsletter, a yearly national meeting, and local chapters. CoG aides covens in becoming recognized churches, with tax exempt status and the right to perform legally binding marriages; it also provides a network of covens that exchange information. Because CoG emphasizes coven autonomy it has not attempted to create paid clergy or staff, although it is in the process of collecting materials from covens on the training of priestesses and priests. CoG is only one of several organizations that is involved with the spread of information. The Reclaiming Collective, which developed about twelve years ago around Starhawk's coven in the San Francisco Bay area, relies on volunteers to teach classes, run two-week intensive training sessions, and publish a newsletter (Adler 1986:413; Orion 1995:260).

ESC is clearly an important part of the Neo-Pagan information network. It helped to continue the debate about paid clergy through the publication in *FireHeart* of a four-part debate among five prominent Neo-Pagans: Andras Corban Arthen of ESC; Isaac Bonewits, founder of the largest Neo-Pagan Druid organization in the United States; Judy Harrow, a high priestess of a coven in the Gardnerian tradition and a former officer of CoG; Oriethyia, a radical lesbian, feminist, and Witch; Sam Webster, a Wiccan and theology student who at the time of the debates hoped to become a Unitarian Universalist minister. By bringing the issue of establishing a professional staff or clergy into the public dialogue, ESC is also contributing to the development of normative isomorphism. The ESC newsletter specifically addressed the controversy surrounding Andras and Deirdre's attempt to create a financial base for their organization; however, debates have continued about the larger issue of what type of institutional changes—if any—should be implemented in Wicca.

In the debates in *FireHeart* both Andras Arthen and Isaac Bonewits argue for the creation of a paid clergy within Wicca. Judy Harrow and Oriethyia contend that the development of paid clergy is inappropriate for Neo-Paganism. Sam Webster defines himself as sitting firmly on the fence, arguing that there is no need for a Neo-Pagan clergy within the coven system, but that some individuals should, like himself, become trained and join other organizations, such as the Unitarian Universalist Association.

The break along gender lines—the men speaking for the need for greater organization and the women arguing against the development of a bureaucracy—is neither accidental nor universal. All-women's groups are the most ideologically opposed to the development of any form of hierarchy, although there is a movement even in these groups toward requiring more rigorous and consistent training (Griffin 1996). Judy Harrow is not a member of an all-women's group, but rather a Gardnerian high priestess of a coven that includes men and women. Ms. Harrow is concerned that the development of paid clergy will result in a shift away from the coven structure to the development of congregations.

> This is the problem: the typical small intimate coven traditionally has no more than thirteen members. That's certainly not enough to support a priest/ess. But a group large enough to do so will also need meeting space larger than a living room. Supporting the building requires even more contributors. We'd soon be caught in the trap of cash addiction. . . . Next those who could contribute more would also be having a greater say in congregational decisions. This loss of equality within the group, along with the loss of intimacy, would erode belief that the God/dess lives in each of us. (Harrow 1991:35)

Ms. Harrow concedes that clergy of more traditional religions have training that is lacking in Neo-Paganism. On the one hand, she believes the cost of having traditionally trained and supported clergy would require changes too great within Witchcraft. On the other hand, she argues that the Witchcraft community has begun a process of making the training for priestesses more rigorous. Sam Webster, who initially appears to be agreeing with Judy Harrow and Oriethyia, eventually joins the other two men in arguing that paid clergy would improve the training of members of the community and help legitimize the religion.

Andras Arthen and Isaac Bonewits, both of whom are the heads of large organizations, note that the increasing number of new converts to Neo-Paganism is making it difficult for neophytes to be adequately trained through covens. They are concerned that individuals, after reading a few books, will declare themselves Witches and priestesses or priests and attempt to train others with their little knowledge. Both Arthen and Bonewits are troubled about the ill effects this will have on the larger Neo-Pagan community: they fear that poorly trained high priestesses or priests will become burned out magically and will bring the legitimacy of the religion into question.

Inanna Arthen argues that without a larger organizational structure Neo-Pagans "keep reinventing the wheel." As an example, she described finding a magazine when she was on vacation in Maine.

> The leading article in the Pagan journal was the Wiccan Rede ["Do as thou will as long as thou harm none"] revisited—and I thought, my gosh, it has been twenty years since *Green Egg* and we are still publishing these articles. The Wiccan Rede now has handicapped access and asphalt sidewalks because it has been visited so often. Can we develop any kind of consistency with people coming into this having some knowledge of what went before? And it's not happening—everyone comes into Paganism and makes it up all over again. It's almost still at the starting gate, and that to me is very frustrating. (Inanna Arthen Interview 1996)

Inanna's concern is twofold. First, she worries that older members of the community will become alienated from the newcomers and stop attending festivals; then the magical and spiritual knowledge of the older members of the community will be lost. Second, she hopes that Neo-Paganism will take its place with more mainstream religions. To do this she believes the religion needs educated spokespeople who are seminary trained and well versed in theological issues. In the debates about the paid clergy Isaac Bonewits similarly argues, "Many of the topics that would be covered in a mainstream ministerial training program are absent [from the training of Neo-Pagan clergy]: . . . It's no wonder that mainstream clergy find it difficult to take our clergy seriously—not only do we belong to religions they've been taught to denigrate, most of us don't have a quarter of the specialized education and training that they believe is necessary in order to be ordained" (Bonewits 1991:37).

The concern for greater legitimacy and recognition within the larger religious community may at first seem odd for a religion that in the United States grew out of the counterculture. However, the early adherents of this religion are today increasingly middle-aged professionals and parents who are seeking consistency and legitimacy in their religious practice.

NEO-PAGANS AND THE UNITARIAN UNIVERSALIST ASSOCIATION

The development of CUUPs and the increase of Neo-Pagans who are joining the Unitarian Universalist Association are indicative of Neo-Pagans' search for legitimacy and consistency. The interest in Neo-Paganism among the Unitarian Universalists grew out of the quest by women within the association for a feminist form of spirituality. In 1986 the UUA women's federation published teaching materials on goddess spirituality—*Cakes for the Queen of Heaven*— which were subsequently published for a general audience (Ranck 1995). This book has been superseded within the UUA by new teaching materials—*Rise Up and Call Her Name*—that include videos and music tapes as well as a text (Fisher 1994). CUUPs was founded in 1987 as an independent affiliate organization of the Unitarian Universalist Association by the Reverend Lesley Phillips, Linda Pinti, and a small group of women[9] "who had discovered the importance of traditions that honor women and the earth. Membership increased by leaps and bounds. . . . Men began to join too out of deep concern for the destruction of the earth—and I think also because the rituals gave them an opportunity to express themselves in costume and dance" (Ranck 1996).

The stated purpose of the organization is "to enrich and strengthen the religious pluralism of UUism by promoting the study and practice of contemporary Pagan and Earth and nature-centered spirituality" (UUA 1996b). CUUPs reorganized in 1996 with a new board of directors. The organization continues to gain new membership. Unlike the early members, who discovered goddess spirituality after joining the association, some of the newer CUUPs members have joined the group and the association from the Neo-Pagan community.

It is impossible to determine the exact number of Neo-Pagans who are members of the Unitarian Universalist Association. There are nearly seven hundred active members of CUUPs, and a larger number of associate members who receive a newsletter; but whose names are not on the membership list and who cannot vote. In a telephone interview Jerrie Hildebrand, the CUUPs public relations representative, stated that some Neo-Pagans become associate members because they do not want their names on the membership list, which is public.[10] They fear the negative repercussions of openly defining themselves as Neo-Pagans. Other Neo-Pagans have joined the Unitarian Universalist Association but have not become members of CUUPs. For instance, Inanna Arthen is active in her local Unitarian Universalist congregation, where she is doing her student ministry and has preached on Neo-Pagan themes, but she has not joined CUUPs. Some Neo-Pagans, like the Mayfires who were mentioned in chapter 5, join a Unitarian Universalist congregation without explicitly acknowledging their Neo-Pagan practices to other members of their congregation. The Mayfires continue to celebrate Neo-Pagan holidays in their home, at Neo-Pagan gatherings, or with Wiccan friends and their covens. As the Mayfires' initial reason for joining the Unitarian Universalists was to provide a safe religious affiliation for their children, they make a clear demarcation between the two practices.

Although the number of Neo-Pagans within the Unitarian Universalist Association is a small percentage of all Unitarian Universalists and also of all Neo-Pagans, the development of CUUPs is significant. The Unitarian Universalist Association provides one avenue through which routinization may occur for Neo-Pagans whether or not they are members of the association. Several Neo-Pagans I spoke to believe that the Unitarian Universalist Association, with its long and respected history, well-developed bureaucracy, church buildings, capital funds, and the publishing houses of Beacon Press and Skinner Press, have many assets that could be helpful to the Neo-Pagan community. As was seen in the debates surrounding EarthSpirit Community's aborted capital fund drive, it is difficult to raise money for the establishment of a bureaucracy or for buildings within the Neo-Pagan community. Inanna Arthen contends, "The vision that the people who are in the group [trying to develop a church or independent financial base] had was not as attractive as they thought it should be, or thought it would be to people who were not part of the group because it was not inclusive in the way that they thought it should be or could be viewed by people outside this group" (Inanna Arthen Interview 1996). According to Inanna, this is true not only for EarthSpirit Community, but also for other groups with which she is acquainted. She feels that those outside an inner group find it difficult to participate in the vision because there is nothing concrete, such as a building or an established bureaucracy, in which individuals can invest. She argues that this problem is magnified because there is within Neo-Paganism no equivalent to the biblical injunction to tithe. But as she notes, an organization cannot survive in the long term on individuals' paying for events. She sees this as a quandary for the Neo-Pagan community, as without funding it is impossible to have a stable enough structure to successfully solicit donations.

The Neo-Pagans who join the Unitarian Universalists are participating in an organization with a history and with assets, an institution to which individuals can feel comfortable contributing. The Unitarian Universalists do not have a statement of faith but instead affirm a set of purposes and principles and share sources of inspiration. Some congregations are Christian in orientation, others more humanist, while still others are eclectic. The development of CUUPs and the addition of the "spiritual teachings of Earth-centered tradition which celebrate the sacred circle of life and instruct us to live in harmony with the rhythms of nature" (UUA 1996a) to the sources of inspiration for the Unitarian Universalists makes the association an appealing religious affiliation for Neo-Pagans.

Jerrie Hildebrand believes her organization can be of service to the larger Neo-Pagan community. For example, she notes that children's educational materials and materials about men's mysteries are being created under the leadership of a Neo-Pagan Unitarian Universalist minister. These materials will be available to members of the association, as well as interested individuals. Jerrie Hildebrand asserts that Neo-Pagans can, in turn, "bring the heart back into the UUA, which has become too heady" (Jerrie Hildebrand Interview 1996). Margot Adler, who is on the board of CUUPs, similarly notes, "the pagan community has brought to UUism the joy of ceremony and a lot of creative and artistic ability that will leave the denomination with a richer liturgy and a bit more juice and mystery" (1996:87). Neo-Pagans and Unitarian Universalists share a number of similarities. Both are noncredal religions that rely on several sources for spiritual inspiration and both groups strongly emphasize issues of social justice and individual conscience.

There are also some fundamental differences. Suzanne Meyer, a Unitarian Universalist minister in New Orleans, suggests that her religion has traditionally been "perhaps the quintessential modern religion" (quoted in Ross 1996:29). The Unitarian Universalist Association has been "known as a home for people who would put their faith in reason and social ac-

tion, rather than in God" (G. Niebuhr 1996:28). In describing her participation in the freshman seminar at Harvard, Inanna Arthen summed up
the differences she felt between her own spirituality and those of her Unitarian Universalist classmates:

> It's a highly varied group, so in my section along with a num-
> ber of UUs and me there were a couple of people from very
> evangelical traditions. . . . What was really funny was I found
> myself in discussion after discussion supporting them or say-
> ing things that they then spoke up and supported me in versus
> the Unitarians who were being much more humanistic. So we
> would be talking about different issues of ministry and I would
> be saying but what about the spiritual aspect and what about
> the fact that if you are a spiritual person and you have what I
> would call magical work and they would call religious work
> and you want to do this on an ongoing basis because there is
> not support for this in the culture because the culture is so
> secular. These guys are all on one side of the team speaking of
> how hard it is to be a spiritual person in a secular world and
> for the UUs this was not such a big issue. (Inanna Arthen Inter-
> view 1996)

Unitarian Universalism is, however, in the process of change, of which
the incorporation of Neo-Pagans is only one part. Some Unitarian Universalists experience an increasing desire for spirituality and ceremony (Ross
1996; G. Niebuhr 1996). Rev. Suzanne Meyer contends that the religion
is changing as the culture itself moves from a modern to a postmodern
society. Rev. Scott Alexander, a Boston-based minister, summed up those
differences by suggesting, "The last generation of Unitarian-Universalists
were fleeing Methodism, Roman Catholicism, Judaism. . . . What this
generation is fleeing is the emptiness of the culture" (quoted in G. Niebuhr
1996:28). The changes occurring within Unitarian Universalism are not
without conflict—and in some congregations there is a growing tension
among members.

This tension is greatest between those within the association who
are "at either end of the theological spectrum—either Pagan or Christian" as Marjorie Bowens-Wheatly put it (quoted in Ross 1996:35). For
congregations in the Bible Belt especially, friction may arise between Neo-
Pagan Unitarian Universalists and local churches. One example is the
controversy that developed between the Unitarian Universalist and Baptist churches over the interaction between CUUPs members and a few
children in Beaumont, Texas. The local newspaper reported that the chil-

dren wandered into the Spindletop Unitarian churchyard from a Little League baseball field. One of the children was allegedly sprinkled with glitter, which was described by the Unitarian Universalist Pagans as fairy dust (Stewart 1996). A letter written by one of the seven Spindletop Unitarian Pagans in the CUUPs newsletter contended that the CUUPs members were merely doing yard work when the children wandered onto the property (Jones 1996).

In response to the incident, Rev. Rozell of the Baptist church organized a seminar on the occult to which he invited the public; the invitation was broadcast on the local television station. Among those who attended the seminar were the Spindletop minister, Rev. Thompson, who is not a Pagan, and members of the CUUPs chapter. During the presentation Rev. Rozell directly attacked CUUPs and the Spindletop congregation and used unauthorized footage of the Spindletop Neo-Pagans' esabat rituals. The Unitarian Universalists who attended the seminar had been enjoined by representatives of the Baptist church to remain silent under threat of arrest. After he spoke out against what he described as untruths about his church and parishioners, Rev. Thompson was arrested by law enforcement officers who were in attendance at the seminar (Stewart 1996; Jones 1996). The response of the other members of the Spindletop congregation was mixed. Ruth Doyle, a member of the church for forty years, said, "We don't mind them being pagans, we just don't want them to do it in our backyards" (quoted in Stewart 1996). The minister, on the other hand, supported his Neo-Pagan parishioners to the degree of being arrested for their right of spiritual expression.

Some congregations have disagreed about the use of the sanctuary by Unitarian Universalist Pagans for sabbat or esabat rituals. Rev. Beuhrans, the president of the Unitarian Universalist Association, in an interview noted, "We have had some relationships between particular local congregations and local Pagan groups that haven't gone well. A few congregations felt exploited. Pluralism and acceptance is one thing—but the use of the building can be an issue. So can adverse publicity—especially when such publicity seems sought by Neo-Pagans" (Beuhrans Interview 1996).

At its 1996 general assembly the Unitarian Universalist Association amended its sources of inspiration to include earth-based traditions. CUUPs was at the center of the effort to have earth-based religions added to the UUA Principles and Purposes as a source of inspiration (Ranck 1996). However, as one Neo-Pagan notes, "I am very pleased to see that the RE [religious education] curriculum on world religion includes a segment on my chosen religious path. . . . I couldn't help wondering why the RE program can call Hindus Hindus, Buddhists

Buddhists and Muslims Muslims yet we pagans have to be euphemized under the heading 'Nature-Based Religionists'" (White 1996:13). For some Neo-Pagans Unitarian Universalism has provided a spiritual home. It is a church in which they can comfortably raise their children, because it is a recognized church that their children, without negative repercussions, can acknowledge membership in at their schools, and because it allows exposure to a number of different religious traditions or inspirations. Neo-Pagan Unitarian Universalist parents feel that they are providing their children with a basis for choosing their own spiritual path. Furthermore, the political activism of the Unitarian Universalists is consistent with the political concerns of many Neo-Pagans. Margot Adler reflects the sentiments of many Unitarian Universalist Neo-Pagans in speaking of her own participation in CUUPs and the Unitarian Universalist Association. "I guess I chose UUism because I need to live in balance. I can do all those wonderful, earth-centered spiritual things. But I also need to be a worldly down-to-earth person in a complicated world" (1996:18).

Dr. Elisabeth McGregor, a trustee of the Unitarian Universalist Association, believes that Neo-Pagans have "enriched the liturgical life of the denomination, which tended to be a bit sparse and intellectual." However, she also sees the potential for—and in some instances the beginnings of—problems arising if "people see themselves as Pagans first, UUs incidentally and are not interested in the range of philosophy and spirituality represented by the Judeo-Christian tradition and the rest of UUism. Enthusiasts of any persuasion can be narrow, and it's that narrowness that runs into trouble in UU circles" (McGregor 1996).

It is still too early to know how many Neo-Pagans will become members of the Unitarian Universalist Association and the effect this will have on both religions. The small number of Neo-Pagans who have joined the Unitarian Universalists have already had an impact on the organization—through the addition of earth-based religions as one of the sources of inspiration, changes in religious education programs, and the employment of Unitarian Universalist Neo-Pagan ministers. To date only one Unitarian Universalist congregation was completely Neo-Pagan focused; and it is no longer in existence. There is concern within the association that Neo-Paganism not become a religion within a religious affiliation. To the degree that Wicca becomes subsumed under the auspices of the Unitarian Universalist Association it will be changed dramatically, as the CUUPs members and other Neo-Pagans join in worship and fellowship with other Unitarian Universalists and become part of their pluralism. Although the Unitarian Universalist Association offers one route for Neo-Pagans to bureaucratization and legitimacy, it is doubtful that it will ever be the only alternative open to Wicca.

ALTERNATIVE ORGANIZATIONS

Inanna Arthen, although presently a member of a Unitarian Universalist congregation, does not intend to become a minister within that tradition. She stated that her interest in attending Harvard Divinity School was to develop the professional skills and gain the credentials to create a Neo-Pagan church. She envisions the church as following the Neo-Pagan cycles of sabbats and esabats, as well as having Sunday services. She notes that the regular gathering on Sunday of a congregation helps to foster a community. She sees a lack within Neo-Paganism:

> Pagan groups have not yet organized themselves to the point where they are able to offer that degree of community to people whose interest lies not in being part of mystery religion and pushing their boundaries and really doing intense magical work—but people who simply want to practice a religion that is not a Christian religion—who are drawn to a very earth centered polytheistic, ecstatic, participatory religion and come to the open circles to get that, but who want more. (Inanna Arthen Interview 1996)

Inanna Arthen's vision of a Neo-Pagan church has similarities to a Christian congregation—a place where individuals can come for worship, join in study groups, and participate in fellowship. She wants each person to participate to the degree they feel comfortable—attending only on Sundays, or some Sundays, or only the major sabbat rituals, or becoming a more central person within the group. Study groups might develop among those members of the congregation who want to "push their boundaries and participate in shape shifting." Inanna believes that there are many people who feel drawn to Neo-Paganism and want to express their spirituality in this medium, but who do not want to make the commitment of time and energy that a coven requires.

Inanna Arthen is not alone in her vision of a Neo-Pagan church on the street corner. Throughout the United States there are groups that have attempted to open churches. Most of these have been funded through the operation of small occult stores. Inanna mentioned one such church in Nashua, New Hampshire, that had recently closed due to economic difficulties. Dependence on a small business to maintain a religious organization gives rise to a number of problems. First, occult supply and bookstores, like all small businesses, have a high rate of failure. Second, separating the needs of the business from those of the religious practices can be difficult. The dependence on congregants' making purchases from the shop has the potential to warp religious practices or at least raises concerns about the church's merely being a way to support the business.

Before the closing of the Circle of Light coven, Arachne and Gabriel began to collaborate with members of six other covens to create a church. The group is in the process of becoming a legally recognized church and developing an organizational structure—that is, establishing guidelines for membership, election of leaders, and development of standing committees. They are presently working out of their homes but hope eventually to have land and a building for holding festivals and teaching classes. When I last spoke to them they were uncertain about how they would finance a church building and land. Finances remain the major issue in the creation of Wiccan churches. Inanna Arthen, at least initially, aspires to finance her church by combining it with a public service program, such as a shelter for battered women, which she hopes to support through government or charitable grants. As she nears completion of her degree, she is becoming more concerned about how she will fund her vision.

Routinization and Its Detractors

There is no single avenue to routinization within Wicca, although it is clear that many of its participants have a strong impetus to develop a more structured form of worship. The shift toward greater homogeneity is the outgrowth of several forces. One is the standardization of religious practices that results from the spread of information through the growth of technology and the increased participation by adherents in Neo-Pagan gatherings. Another is the birth of children to Witches, a development that is nudging the religion in the direction of greater routinization and a search for more legitimacy.

In part, the aging of the religion and its adherents has increased interest in the creation of paid clergy. Andras and Deirdre's attempt to be paid as administrators for their work at ESC came after the birth of their son. Forces against the development of a trained and paid clergy exist particularly, although not exclusively, among Dianic and other all-women's groups. Those who oppose the development of paid clergy or staff worry that it will result in elitism, as only those with the economic resources will be able to attend seminary. They also fear the development of a hierarchy and dogma. A man in his mid-thirties summarized this position in "The Pagan Census": "The Pagan movement will sell its soul (so to speak) if it gets too organized. I think religion is a very personal experience to be shared only among close friends/lovers. . . . 'Experts,' 'authorities,' 'religious leaders' are all bad signs! . . . I understand the need and desire for community and sharing ideas. However, such connections need to be grass-roots meetings of peers" (H. Berger and A. Arthen n.d.: 2509).

The voices of dissension will not disappear from the debate. There will always be those within Neo-Paganism who oppose the development of bureaucratization and who will continue to work as either solitaries or within a coven. H. Niebuhr (1929) suggests that churches tend to spawn sects, only in turn to have those sects become new churches, which eventually develop sects. Warner (1993:1065) notes that in the United States there is an alternation between increased "centripetal and centrifugal tendencies." Even as Wicca routinizes, both sects and centrifugal tendencies will continue. Covens will form and meet in homes. They may, as Inanna Arthen complains, "reinvent the wheel," or they may react against the routinization that has developed in the religion. Ready access to the Internet, desktop publishing, and participation in festivals will make their voices heard. Covens, churches, bureaucracies, and Unitarian Universalist Pagans will coexist within Wicca in the United States.

The routinization that is occurring in Wicca is in some ways following Weber's predictions about the routinization of charisma. Spontaneity and creativity of religious expression are being replaced by more standardized rituals and practices. At least the rudiments of a clergy/administrative staff are forming. The clergy, however, rather than acting as the bearers of routinized charisma or the interpreters of the word, are people who are knowledgeable about organizing a coven, adjudicating differences, or running a workshop. Routinization of this new religion follows the model of homogenization of other organizations in late modernity. Computer networks, workshops, books, and magazines all contribute to the growth in mutual awareness, interactions, and similarity of characteristics among groups. The desire for professionalization has crept into Wicca. The power that exists within the religion is fractured, but nonetheless a religion that prides itself on spontaneity and playfulness is aging and becoming more standardized. Curiously like the disciples who attempted to capture the charisma of the prophetic period only to recreate a priest class, Neo-Pagans' attempt to capture the spontaneity and creativity of their early religious expression is shaping a new form of routinization.

CHAPTER 7

Conclusion

The practices and aging of the new religious movement of Witchcraft and Neo-Paganism in the United States—an earth-based, feminist form of spirituality—have been explored in this book. Most of the adherents of this religion are white, middle class, and well educated. Wicca, which originated in Great Britain in the 1930s, migrated to the United States in the 1960s. This amorphous religion's lack of a central bureaucracy or dogma that defines orthodoxy has led to the development of many different groups and traditions. My focus has been on Wiccan groups in the United States that include both women and men. Other scholars (Finley 1991; Neitz 1991) have suggested that all-women's Witchcraft groups are sociologically more significant than groups that involve men as well as women, because they provide a cultural resource for the creation of feminist spirituality within mainstream religions. To the contrary, I have argued that inclusive groups will ultimately have a greater impact because their involvement of entire families and their stronger interest in creating organizations and churches will facilitate the survival of their religion. Furthermore, inclusive groups provide alternative gender roles for both men and women.

Unlike Orion (1995), who suggests that Wicca is a postmodern religion, I have asserted that Wicca should be viewed within the context of late modernity. Although the playfulness of the religious practice, the pastiche of rituals from diverse cultures, and the questioning of rationality makes Wicca appear at first glance to be postmodern, closer examination reveals that the religion has not rejected the Enlightenment project. Wicca has instead stood the Enlightenment on its head by applying the methodological skepticism of the Enlightenment to rationalism itself. My analysis of Wicca as a religion of late modernity has been guided by Beckford (1984, 1992a, 1992b). Although he does not specifically discuss Wicca, my view of this religion coincides with his model of religions of late modernity: as incorporating a holistic image of the universe; the view that individuals are not separate from, but part of, nature; the notion that personal and cosmic changes are intertwined; the acceptance of personal transformation as a necessary part of changes in the social world; and the belief in the fusion of the personal and the political.

My analysis of Wicca within the context of late modernity has been informed by Giddens (1984, 1987, 1990, 1991, 1992). He discusses the development of self-identity, life-politics, and the role of friendship in late modernity—all of which have resonance in the Witchcraft movement. Within Wicca, self-transformation occurs through rituals, magical incantations, and participation in the Neo-Pagan community—practices that foster an atmosphere of self-reflection and change. The creation and re-creation of the self in Wicca is consistent with the requirements in late modernity for a Promethean self. Along with Giddens and Beckford, Gergen (1991) notes that the sense of a stable self-identity through a lifetime is consistent with the life world of small communities and an earlier era of slower change. Late modernity demands of all people, particularly the urban middle class, an ability to change lifestyles, jobs, or even professions.

The self is not created in isolation, but through friendships and communities of choice. As Giddens reminds us, intimate relationships in modernity are pure relationships that are not embedded in tradition, blood ties, or economic relationships, but instead are an outgrowth of mutual interests and concerns. The coven is the primary avenue for training neophytes to be members of the Neo-Pagan community. Although information about ritual techniques and magical incantations is available in books and journals and on the Internet, it is in the cocoon of the coven that most Witches are trained to be members of the larger Neo-Pagan community. The friendships that develop in the coven help to foster a mystical worldview, feminist and ecological political concerns, and other lifestyle choices. Covens tend to be short-lived, in part because they are based on pure relationships that are not embedded in economic or political alliances. Furthermore, although covens have many of the attributes of a congregation, they are less stable because they have neither a church building nor a bureaucracy separate from the participants. Although covens are unstable, the people who compose them, who often separate in anger, also come back together to form new covens, participate in rituals, or do magical workings.

The covens, their members, and solitary practitioners are encompassed by the larger Neo-Pagan community. I have argued that Neo-Pagans should be viewed as a community, although they do not meet the definition of a traditional community, which is based on face-to-face long-term relationships. Instead, Witches form a community of interest. The development of desktop publishing, the Internet, and the ability of people to travel great distances in short periods of time have resulted in communities' forming around mutual interests and political concerns instead of blood ties, ethnicity, or locality. Although the Witchcraft community is amorphous with unclear boundaries, it helps to define ritual practices, beliefs, and behaviors—taking the place, in some ways, of the denomination of other religions.

Neo-Pagans have created a community of memory based on the myth of returning to or continuing a pan-European pre-Christian religion. The reinterpretation or creation of the past from the present is not unique to Witches. However, what does distinguish the Witches as members of late modernity is their self-conscious creation of this myth. Most Witches acknowledge that their religion is relatively new, but they nonetheless believe their practices to be linked to pre-Enlightenment religious activities and to those individuals who were executed as witches in the early modern period. The mythical link to lay healers, magicians, and those executed in the witch trials provides a basis for the creation of community and an alternative worldview to that of modern rationality—which is perceived as having incorporated into its premises patriarchy and domination of nature.

Raphael (1996), while acknowledging Witchcraft as a religion of late modernity, has questioned its ability to provide what she believes are the essential elements of a religion—a moral code and compensation for life's losses. I have argued, to the contrary, that although Wiccans espouse a tolerance of alternative lifestyles, ethics, and even interpretations of the goddesses and gods, moral issues are becoming reembedded through the life politics of environmental responsibility, gender equality, freedom of sexual expression, and tolerance of diversity.

Giddens distinguishes between emancipatory politics—the battles for human rights—and life politics that grow out of lifestyle choices. The two forms of politics are not exclusive and often overlap. However, life politics are a direct outgrowth of lifestyle choices of late modernity. Giddens contends that it is through life politics that moral issues, which have been subjugated in modernity by relativism and the questioning of all knowledge claims, are becoming reembedded. Within Wicca the life politics of feminism, environmentalism, and sexual freedom that are interwoven with magical practices, rituals, and chants are fostering the reembedding of moral issues.

Witchcraft is in the process of change. The early adherents who were in their twenties when they joined Wicca in the late 1960s and early 1970s are now middle-aged professionals with children. The birth of children to members of the community has resulted in a reevaluation of the religion and its practices. From its inception, the religion was viewed as "the old religion" and, contradictorily, as a spiritual path a person may choose. Initially this contradiction was not apparent, as participants were *choosing* to "return" to the "old ways." However, an "old religion" has traditions that are passed down through the generations. Children are not spiritual seekers but recipients of their parents' religious practices. In books, journals, and conversations on the Internet and at festivals, the appropriateness and correct manner of introducing Wicca to children are discussed. A body of literature is developing to teach Wicca to children.

The literature that is being produced to teach Neo-Paganism to children is part of the process of routinization within this new religion. Information about how to organize a coven, write a ritual, and perform magical rites have been shared in books and journals since the beginning of the American Neo-Pagan movement in the 1960s. However, initially there was a good deal of personal innovation. The Internet and attendance at festivals have led to an increasing similarity among adherents in their ritual practices, interpretations, and magical acts.

The routinization occurring in this religion is consistent with DiMaggio and Powell's examination of the systemization of other organizations in late modernity (1983). They suggest that routinization in the business world is the result of increased coercive, mimetic, and normative isomorphism. Coercive isomorphism, which occurs when institutions respond to government regulation, does not play a significant part in the routinization of Wicca. However, as I have shown, mimetic and normative isomorphism are important in understanding the routinization that is occurring in Wicca.

Mimetic isomorphism occurs because of the uncertainty involved in creating new rituals, celebrations, magical rites, and covens. Individuals seek out information from others who have written sabbat rituals, created wiccaning rites, and formed covens when they are attempting to create their own. Normative isomorphism is the result of increased professionalism. There is a growing concern among Neo-Pagans that their religion be viewed by the larger society as legitimate. This desire for legitimacy is fueled in part by parents' anxiety that their religious affiliation not adversely affect their children and in part by the aging of the early participants.

The development of churches, the involvement of Neo-Pagans in the Unitarian Universalist Association, and the attendance of Neo-Pagans at seminaries illustrate Neo-Pagans' striving to become more mainstream and their desire for increased professionalism.

Within Wicca there is an ongoing debate about the benefits and disadvantages of routinization. While some individuals are fighting for the development of paid clergy or bureaucrats, others are opposing it. The opponents of such changes within their religion fear the development of elitism and the loss of spontaneity and creativity. Although I see a growth in routinization in the religion, the voices of dissent will not be quieted. They will continue to produce books and to write in Neo-Pagan journals and on the Internet. Individuals will continue to practice in covens or as solitaries. At the same time, however, Neo-Pagan churches and bureaucracies will grow, and that growth will help to define ritual and magical practices.

Although the routinization of this new religion has some similarities to Weber's concept of the routinization of charisma, there are significant differences. Most notably, the justification for the creation of paid staff or clergy is not based on those individuals' religious purity or ability to interpret the words of the prophet. Instead, Neo-Pagans insist that the need for people with professional or bureaucratic knowledge to serve a larger and more diverse Neo-Pagan population justifies the growth of routinization. Like other aspects of this religion, routinization must be understood as occurring within the context of late modernity. The forces that are affecting Wicca are affecting all organizations in late modernity.

Robbins and Bromley (1992) have suggested that new religious movements are social laboratories for alternative cultural patterns and lifestyles. They mention Wicca as providing alternative gender roles for women. I have suggested that Neo-Pagans are also experimenting with feminist notions of male gender roles. As a religion that not only grows out of late modernity but that also embraces its notions of relativism, globalism, and skepticism, Wicca is a social laboratory for the development of friendship, community, routinization, and the reembedding of moral issues in late modernity, as well as for the experimentation with gender roles for women and men.

The Future

Wicca is at a crossroads. In Robbins's review of research on new religious movements, he identifies three components that determine the long-term viability of a new religion: the successful socialization of children into the religious beliefs and practices of their parents; the development of an organizational structure; and accommodation between the religion and the larger society (1988:110–13). Wiccan groups are in the process of addressing each of these challenges to survival, although they do not see the imminent collapse of their religion. To the contrary, they are concerned about accommodating the increasing numbers of new participants at festivals and within the community. The debates within Wicca about child rearing and increased routinization are occurring because of the more immediate problems of raising children, providing training for priestesses and priests, and maintaining a spiritual community for a growing number of people. Nonetheless, successful responses to the issues of socialization of the next generation, organizational structure, and legitimacy will determine the religion's fate in future generations.

Although Wicca is responding to the same challenges to its long-term survival as other new religions, its responses are informed by its being a religion of late modernity. For instance, Neo-Pagan parents do not believe that they possess the one and only path that their children should follow. Neo-Pagan parents accept the notion, common in late modernity and particularly among the middle class, that each child is a unique individual whose self-development should be fostered. Wiccans also adhere to the notion that all truth claims—even their own—are open to question. At this point the future of the religion and its adherents is not clear. Wicca has been affected by the birth of children and rudimentary professionalism and routinization; however, the full impact of these changes will not be felt for a decade or two.

I have described the effect that Wiccan children are having on the religion, but I did not discuss in detail the effect on children of being raised as Wiccans. This is because very few of the second generation have grown to adulthood. How many of them will rebel against their parents' spirituality to become secular humanists, members of mainstream religions, or members of another new religion, and how many will remain Witches? Will being raised in the magical world of Wicca affect the life chances (that is, the probability of reaching their life goals), worldview, or self-perception of these children? If members of the second generation do become Wiccans, what effect will this have on the religion? Will they become "sabbat Neo-Pagans," who join with their family and friends only for the major holidays, or will they remain committed to the notion of continual self-transformation through magic? As the religion and its participants age, answers to these questions will become more apparent.

In a religion that grew out of the counterculture and that questions all authority, the development of churches and bureaucracies would appear to be anathema. However, an increasing number of Neo-Pagans are working towards the development of a professional paid clergy, with training and credentials similar to that of mainstream religions' clergy. The skepticism about clergy, bureaucracies, and hierarchy has made it difficult for Neo-Pagans to find a financial basis for the creation of funded organizations with paid staff. Although some Neo-Pagans support the idea of paid clergy in principle, will they be willing to participate in making substantial donations to capital funds? If there are no successful fund drives, will there be alternative methods of purchasing buildings or land and supporting a bureaucracy?

One of the alternatives to the development of a separate denomination or denominations of Wicca has been the inclusion of Neo-Pagans in the Unitarian Universalist Association. Although initially the Covenant of the Unitarian Universalist Pagans (CUUPs) grew out of the women's spirituality groups that developed within the Unitarian Universalist Association, it is attracting into its organization Neo-Pagans who had not previously been members of the Unitarian Universalists. Men have joined the organization both from inside the association and from the Neo-Pagan community. CUUPs made a major transition in 1996 with the election of a new board of directors: previously the organization was headed by its founders, Rev. Lesley Phillips and Linda Pinti.

The Unitarian Universalist Association, which has property, church buildings, publishing houses, and a professional bureaucracy and clergy, offers an established organization to the Neo-Pagans who join. In some ways Neo-Paganism and Unitarian Universalism are similar—both claim inspiration from a number of sources, both advocate tolerance, and both are politically concerned. However, there are also tensions between Neo-Pagans and some of the older members of the Unitarian Universalist Association. Neo-Paganism is a religion of late modernity; Unitarian Universalism is the quintessential modern rationalist religion. There is a movement among some Unitarian Universalists for greater spirituality (G. Niebuhr 1996). The magical and spiritual expression of Wicca, however, may be too radical for many Unitarian Universalists.

If CUUPs becomes one avenue for the routinization of Wicca, it will be interesting to observe how both Neo-Paganism and Unitarian Universalism are changed. Neo-Pagans may be able to become a "religion within a religion" in the Unitarian Universalist Association. The one attempt at a Neo-Pagan Unitarian Universalist congregation did not succeed; however, as more Neo-Pagans join the Unitarian Universalists, there may be enough members to support their own congregations. This would create tension within the Unitarian Universalist Association. Although the association acknowledges and supports diversity among its congregations or fellowships, it does not want to become a bifurcated religion.

Inanna Arthen, who is presently completing her Master's of Divinity degree at Harvard University, and other Neo-Pagan individuals and groups are attempting to find alternative funding to create churches or national organizations. It is still unclear whether they will succeed; but some members of the religion clearly have a strong impetus to develop a congregational structure.

As Witches move toward greater legitimacy and visibility, tensions between them and more fundamentalist religions may grow. The conflict between the Unitarian Universalist Pagans in Texas and their Baptist neighbors was evidence of such tensions. There are also countervailing trends of acceptance of Neo-Paganism as a religion among more mainstream religions. One example was the participation of Neo-Pagans in the Parliament of World's Religions in Chicago in 1993. Although controversial, their participation "was indicative of the opening up of the religious 'market' at the Parliament" (Roberts 1995:122). What alliances and conflicts between Neo-Pagans and other religions will the future hold? Will Witches find themselves in conflict with more fundamentalist religions and allied with more liberal religions? Or will the emphasis on a spiritual and magical worldview shared by Witches and some evangelical religions result in their becoming mutually supportive of one another, at least on some issues, while the Witches politically align themselves with more moderate religions on other issues? In a quest to be viewed as a legitimate religion, what accommodations will Wicca need to make? And how will these changes affect the religion?

This book has placed Wicca within the context of late modernity— an era in which many tendencies born in the Enlightenment have come to fruition. In particular it is a religion that is based on the questioning of truth claims, an acceptance of the self as constructed, and in which community and friendships based on shared interests and life politics have developed. The transformation of this religion shares similarities to the changes that occurred in other new religions that have survived. However, the manner and form of routinization of Wicca, like other aspects of this religion, is affected by its being self-consciously an outgrowth of late modernity. This book provides a model of the rudimentary transformation of a religion of late modernity. It will be interesting to see both how Wicca ultimately reconstitutes itself and whether other religions of late modernity follow the same model.

NOTES

PREFACE

1. The words Witchcraft, Neo-Paganism, Wicca, Witch, and Neo-Pagan are capitalized throughout this text because they refer to either a religion or its adherents.

2. Women's spirituality groups have attracted women in their thirties and forties.

3. As Andras Corban Arthen is publicly known as a Witch, I have used his real name. Other than published authors, whose names I use as they appear in print, covens and Neo-Pagans, unless otherwise stated, are referred to by pseudonyms throughout this book.

4. These lectures were funded by a grant from the National Endowment for the Humanities. I was asked to give these lectures because I had written my doctoral dissertation on the English witchcraft trials of the early modern period.

5. As there is no evidence that the victims of the witch craze were actually participants in a pre-Christian religion, I have not capitalized the term *witch* when referring to those persecuted in the witch trials of the early modern period.

6. As EarthSpirit is a nationally known Neo-Pagan organization I have used its real name.

7. I have not used a pseudonym for CUUPs.

CHAPTER 1: BACKGROUND

1. The term *thealogy* is used by some Witches and feminist scholars to refer to the study of the beliefs and practices of goddess worshippers, and to differentiate it from *theology*, the study of the belief system of God-oriented religions, most notably, Judaism, Christianity, and Islam.

2. Although Giddens would not consider himself a postmodernist, Rosenau (1992) includes him among the postmodern theorists she discusses. However, I would disagree with her placing him in that group, as one of Giddens's central arguments is that the condition of late or high modernity is an outgrowth of Enlightenment thought.

3. This number is probably high.

4. Bonewits (1989) claims to have introduced this derivation into the Neo-Pagan community.

5. Ben-Yehuda (1985) and Russell (1972, 1980) have similarly noted the development and growth of Satan within Christian theology.

6. Luhrmann (1989) has noted a similar interest in fantasy and science fiction literature among British Witches.

7. Adler (1979, 1986), Bonewits (1989), Kelly (1991), Orion (1995) and Rabinovitch (1996) have all developed categories for different types of Neo-Paganism.

8. Mary-Jo Neitz (1991) has suggested that the terms *feminist Witch* and *Neo-Pagan Witch* be used to describe this division. I prefer the term *Wiccans* to *Neo-Pagan Witches* because it alleviates the confusion between Neo-Pagans and Neo-Pagan Witches.

9. These groups usually are Dianics, the most radically feminist of the Witch-craft groups.

10. I have not capitalized the word *pagan* when referring to the historic religions that were given that label by the early Christians.

11. A variation of this is that the energy you send out is returned tenfold.

12. Kelly (1992) noted that by 1985 fifty thousand copies of Starhawk's first book, *The Spiral Dance* (1979), had been sold.

13. All-women's groups tend to participate in less formalized magic than do inclusive groups.

CHAPTER 2: THE MAGICAL SELF

1. As my fieldnotes were written after the ritual, these may not be the exact words that the participants spoke. They are, however, a close facsimile to what I heard.

2. Beckford (1984) refers to these religions as new religious and healing movements.

3. This is not a pseudonym.

4. This is a common chant within Neo-Pagan rituals.

5. As Laurie Cabot is a public figure, I have used her real name.

6. Particular surveys from the "The Pagan Census" are cited with four-digit numbers in the parenthetical references in the text.

7. Bolen (1984, 1989), a psychiatrist, has suggested this as a psychological method for all women and men.

8. Croning is the celebration of a woman's reaching the third stage of life, the crone. This ritual usually takes place when a women is experiencing meno-pause.

9. In her study of a women's spirituality group in which the participants did not define themselves as Witches, Jacobs (1989) similarly describes rituals devised to heal women who have been sexually and physically abused.

10. This number is based on my reassessment of Kelly's approximation (1992) of 300,000 Neo-Pagans in America to 200,000 and on the percentage of men as determined by "The Pagan Census" and Orion's survey (1995).

CHAPTER 3: THE COVEN

1. This segment of the poem is reproduced from my fieldnotes of March 1987.

2. Starhawk (1979) contends that the coven is like a family. As Robbins (1985) notes, the imagery of an alternative family unit permeates all new religious groups. However, for many of these religions the new "family" takes the place of the participants' families of origin. Within Wicca the metaphor of the family helps to define friendship ties, but is not viewed as a substitute for other family relationships.

3. This is a direct quote from Starhawk (1979).

4. Lakoff was one of the earliest scholars to make a distinction between men's and women's speech patterns. For a fuller discussion of the literature and criticisms of this perspective, see Crawford (1995).

CHAPTER 4: A CIRCLE WITHIN A CIRCLE

1. Life worlds (*Lebenswelt*) is a concept developed by phenomenologists to refer to the assumptions and constructs used by members of a group to interpret or create reality. According to phenomenologists, all knowledge—whether that produces by scientist, sociologists, or the person on the street—is mediated through shared assumptions and categories.

2. I know of one Witch, a member of an old New England family, who may have been related to one of the victims of the witch trials in Salem.

3. Many Witches believe in reincarnation and participate in past-life regressions to learn about their former incarnations.

4. Pike (1996) notes that gender differences are evident in the dances around the campfires. Men are more likely to dance at high speeds and to jump over the fire, while women tend to sway in a meditative trance.

CHAPTER 5: THE NEXT GENERATION

1. This figure is based on the chapter 1 estimate of 200,000 Neo-Pagans living in the United States. The estimate of the number of children is probably low because some Neo-Pagans have more than one child. However, since mothers and fathers may each have completed a survey, both claiming the same children, I have for the purpose of this estimate assumed each of the respondents had only one child.

2. Enough Neo-Pagans have joined the Unitarian Universalist Association for a group, the Covenant of Unitarian Universalist Pagans (CUUPs), to have formed. CUUPs will be discussed in greater detail in chapter 6.

3. Pagans jokingly refer to introductory courses on the craft offered at occult bookstores or adult education centers as Wicca or Witchcraft 101.

4. *HAM* was developed as a journal for Pagan children by an adolescent Neo-Pagan whose father is the editor of *Green Egg,* one of the oldest Pagan jour-

nals in the United States. *HAM* was initially distributed by *Green Egg*. The acronym *HAM* was chosen as a play on Dr. Seuss's children's book *Green Eggs and Ham*.

5. This is the same coven whose naming ritual is described at the beginning of chapter 2. In that chapter I used pseudonyms for their magical names, while in this chapter I have used pseudonyms for their mundane names.

6. This quote is from my fieldnotes written after the ritual. I have tried as much as possible to reproduce the speech as it was presented.

7. The terms *godparents* and *guardians* are also used.

8. I am dependent on written accounts and descriptions by my male informants of boys' puberty rites.

9. The religious right and other groups oppose these changes in sexual mores, family life, and gender roles of late modernity.

10. CoG is a loosely structured national federation of covens or groups that worship the goddesses.

CHAPTER 6: THE ROUTINIZATION OF CREATIVITY

1. Portions of this chapter previously appeared in Helen A. Berger, 1995, "Routinization of Spontaneity," *Sociology of Religion* 56 (1): 49–62.

2. Circle Sanctuary has previously been known as Circle Farm and Circle Network. I have not used a pseudonym for either the organization or its leader, Selena Fox, as they are both well known nationally.

3. CUUPs is an independent affiliate of the UUA; as such it is a financially and legally autonomous organization. However, it must affirm its commitment to the principles of and pay an annual fee to the association.

4. Some traditions, such as that of the Gardnerians, have standardized training for their priests and priestesses.

5. Stark and Bainbridge throughout their text use the term *cult* instead of *new religious movements*. Because *cult* has a negative connotation I prefer the more neutral term *new religious movements*.

6. As was mentioned in the preface an individual can become a member of ESC by paying a fee of $30. In return he or she will receive a newsletter, announcements of upcoming events, and a reduction of the fees to attend those events.

7. If performed by recognized clergy, the handfasting is a legal as well as religious ceremony.

8. I have not used pseudonyms for either Jim Alan or Dennis Carpenter.

9. The materials I received from CUUPs list the organization as having been founded in 1987. According to the UUA Directory of Independent Affiliate Organizations, however, CUUPs was founded in 1985. As their names are in the public domain I have not used pseudonyms for the founders of CUUPs.

10. I have not used a pseudonym for Jerrie Hildebrand.

BIBLIOGRAPHY

Adler, Margot. 1979. *Drawing Down the Moon.* Boston: Beacon Press.

———. 1986. *Drawing Down the Moon: Revised and Expanded.* Boston: Beacon Press.

———. 1992. "Interview." *FireHeart* 5:25–33.

———. 1996. "Why I Am a UU Pagan." *World: The Journal of the Unitarian Universalist Association,* November/December, 14–17.

Aidala, Angela. 1985. "Social change, Gender Roles and New Religious Movements." *Sociological Analysis* 46 (3): 287–14.

Allen, Prudence. 1987. "Two Medieval Views of Woman's Identity: Hildegarde of Bingen and Thomas Aquinas." *Studies in Religion* 16 (1): 21–36.

Arthen, Andras Corban. 1987. "My Lecture Notes From Class on Witchcraft and Magic at the Cambridge Adult Education Center."

———. 1989. "From Roots to Dreams: Pagan Festivals and the Quest for Community." *FireHeart,* Spring: 18–23.

———. 1991a. "An Open Letter to the EarthSpirit Community." *EarthSpirit Community Newsletter,* January, 1–6.

———. 1991b. "Pagan Clergy: A Panel Discussion." *FireHeart* 6:40–42, 44–45.

———. 1992. "Community Forum." *EarthSpirit Community Newsletter,* April, 15–17.

———. 1997. "Of Visions, Changes, and Community." *EarthSpirit Newsletter,* Spring, 1, 3.

Arthen, Deirdre Pulgram. 1992. *Walking with Mother Earth.* West Boxford, Mass.: D & J Publications.

Arthen, Nicholson Daile. 1990. "Light From a Shining Shore." *EarthSpirit Community Newsletter,* October 5–8. (Author subsequently changed her name to Inanna Arthen.)

Athene. 1994. "Letter." *EarthSpirit Community Newsletter,* July, 15.

Balch, Robert. 1988. "Money and Power in Utopia: An Economic History of the Love Family." In *Money and Power in New Religions,* ed. James T. Richardson, 185–222. Lewiston, N.Y.: The Edwin Mellen Press.

Barker, Eileen. 1994. "But Is It a Genuine Religion?" In *Religion and the Social*

Order, vol. 4, ed. Arthur L. Greil and Thomas Robbins. Greenwich, Conn.: JAI Press.

Beckford, James. 1984. "Holistic Imagery and Ethics in New Religious and Healing Movements." *Social Compass* 31:259–72.

———. 1992a. *Religion and Advanced Industrial Society.* London: Routledge.

———. 1992b. "Religion and Modernity, Post-Modernity." In *Religion: Contemporary Issues,* ed. Bryan Wilson. London: Bellew.

Bellah, Robert, Richard Madsen, William M. Sullivan, Ann Swindler, and Steven M. Tipton. 1985. *Habits of the Heart.* New York: Harper and Row.

Ben-Yehuda, Nachman. 1985. *Deviance and Moral Boundaries,* Chicago: University of Chicago Press.

Berger, Helen A. 1994. "Witches and Scientists." *Sociological Viewpoints* 10 (Fall): 56–65.

———. 1995. "Routinization of Spontaneity." *Sociology of Religion* 56 (1): 49–62.

Berger, Helen A., and Andras Corbin Arthen. "The Pagan Census—Qualitative Data."

Berger, Helen A., Andras Corbin Arthen, Evan Leach, and Leigh S. Shaffer. "The Pagan Census—The Statistical Analysis."

Berger, Peter L. 1967. *The Sacred Canopy: Elements of a Sociological Theory of Religion.* Garden City, N.Y.: Doubleday.

Bill (MotherChant Men's Auxiliary). 1991. "Paying the Price of Leadership." *EarthSpirit Community Newsletter,* March, 4–10.

Bird, Fred, and Frances Westley. 1988. "Economic Strategies of the New Religious Movements." In *Money and Power in New Religions,* ed. James T. Richardson, 45–68. Lewiston, N.Y.: The Edwin Mellen Press.

Bolen, Jean S. 1984. *Goddesses in Every Woman: A New Psychology of Women.* San Francisco: Harper and Row.

———. 1989. *Gods in Every Man: A New Psychology of Men's Lives and Loves.* San Francisco: Harper and Row.

Bonewits, Isaac. 1989. *Real Magic.* York Beach, Maine: Samuel Weisner.

———. 1991. "Pagan Clergy: A Panel Discussion." *FireHeart* 6:36–38, 48–50.

Campanelli, Pauline. 1994. *Rites of Passage: The Pagan Wheel of Life.* St. Paul, Minn.: Llewellyn Publications.

Charboneau-Harrison, Karen. 1993. "Raising the Pagan Child." In *Modern Rites of Passage: Witchcraft Today Book Two,* ed. Chas S. Clifton, 43–74. St. Paul, Minn.: Llewellyn Publications.

Cohen, Anthony P. 1985. *The Symbolic Construction of Community.* London: Routledge.

Crawford, Mary. 1995. *Talking Difference: On Gender and Lanuage.* Thousand Oaks, Calif.: Sage.

Curewitz, Sue. 1989. "Pagan Rites of Passages: Puberty." *FireHeart* (Spring/Summer): 24–26, 56.

——. 1990. "Pagan Rites of Passages: A Celebration of Birth." *FireHeart* 5:8–10, 54.

Danzger, M. Herbert. 1989. *Returning to Tradition*. New Haven: Yale University Press.

Darling-Ferns, Zack. 1990. "Youth and Maiden Lovemaking." *How About Magic* 1 (Litha) (4): 10.

DiMaggio, Paul, and Walter Powell. 1983. "The Iron Cage Revisited: Institutional Isomorphism and Collective Rationality in Organizational Fields." in *American Sociological Review* 48 (April): 147–60.

Easlea, Brain. 1980. *Witch-hunting, Magic and the New Philosophy: An Introduction to Debates of the Scientific Revolution, 1450–1750*. Brighton, England: Harvester Press.

Ehrenreich, Barbara, and Deirdre English. 1973. *Witches, Midwives and Nurses: A History of Women Healers*. Old Westbury, N.Y.: The Feminist Press.

Eilberg-Schwartz, Howard. 1989. "Witches of the West: Neo-Paganism and Goddess Worship as Enlightenment Religions." *Journal of Feminist Studies of Religion* 5:77–95.

Eller, Cynthia. 1993. *Living in the Lap of the Goddess: The Feminist Spirituality Movement in America*. New York: Crossroads.

Farrar, Janet, and Stewart Farrar. 1992. "Men and Women in Witchcraft." In *The Modern Craft Movement: Witchcraft Today Book One*, ed. Chas S. Clifton. St. Paul, Minn.: Llewellyn Publications.

Finley, Nancy J. 1991. "Political Activism and Feminist Spirituality." *Sociological Analysis* 52 (4): 349–62.

Fischer, Claude, S. 1982. *To Dwell Among Friends*. Chicago: University of Chicago Press.

Fisher, Elizabeth. 1994. *Rise Up and Call Her Name*. Boston: The Unitarian Universalist Women's Federation.

Friedman, Marilyn. 1995. "Feminism and Modern Friendship: Dislocating the Community." In *Feminism and Community*, ed. Penny A. Weiss and Marilyn Friedman. Philadelphia: Temple University Press.

Galbreath, Robert. 1983. "Explaining Modern Occultism." In *The Occult in America: New Historic Perspectives*, ed. Howard Kerr and Charles L. Crow. Urbana: University of Illinois Press.

Gergen, Kenneth J. 1991. *The Saturated Self: Dilemmas of Identity in Contemporary Life*. New York: Basic Books.

Giddens, Anthony. 1979. *Central Problems in Social Theory: Action, Structure and Contradiction in Social Analysis*. Berkeley: University of California Press.

——. 1984. *The Constitution of Society*. Berkeley: University of California Press.

——. 1987. *Social Theory and Modern Society*. Stanford: Stanford University Press.

——. 1990. *The Consequences of Modernity*. Stanford: Stanford Univeristy Press.

——. 1991. *Modernity and Self Identity: Self and Society in the Late Modern*

Age. Stanford: Stanford University Press.

———. 1992. *The Transformation of Intimacy: Sexuality, Love and Eroticism in Modern Societies.* Stanford: Stanford University Press.

Greil, Arthur L., and Thomas Robbins. 1994. "Introduction: Exploring the Boundaries of the Sacred." In *Religion and the Social Order,* vol. 4, ed. Arthur L. Greil and Thomas Robbins. Greenwich, Conn.: JAI Press.

Greil, Arthur L., and David R. Rudy. 1984. "Social Cocoons: Encapsulation and Identity Formation Organizations." *Sociological Inquiry* 54:260–78.

Griffin, Wendy. 1995. "The Embodied Goddess: Feminist Witchcraft and Female Divinity." *Sociology of Religion* 56 (1): 35–48.

———. 1996. "Heratics: Priestesses-in-Training." Paper presented at the Society for the Scientific Study of Religion meetings in Nashville, Tenn..

Guiley, Rosemary Ellen. 1989. *The Encyclopedia of Witches and Witchcraft.* New York: Facts on File.

Harrow, Judy. 1991. "Pagan Clergy: A Panel Discussion." *FireHeart* 6:35–37, 47–48.

Hawkins, Jaq. 1994. "What Do We Teach Our Children." *Melim: Practical Magick for Today* 5 (4): 1–3.

Held, Virginia. 1995. "Non-Contractual Society." In *Feminism and Community,* ed. Penny A. Weiss and Marilyn Friedman. Philadelphia: Temple University Press.

Hervieu-Leger. 1990. "Religion and Modernity in the French Context: For a New Approach to Secularization." *Sociological Analysis* 51:S15–S25.

Hicks, Brad. "The Burning Times." Pamphlet.

Hillery, George. 1955. "Definitions of Community: Areas of Agreement." *Rural Sociology* 20: 111–23.

Jacobs, Janet. 1989. "The Effects of Ritual Healing on Female Victims of Abuse." *Sociological Analysis* 50:265–79.

———. 1991. "Women-Centered Healing Rites: A Study of Alienation and Reintegration." In *In Gods We Trust,* ed. Thomas Robbins and Dick Anthony, 373–84. New Brunswick, N.J.: Transaction Press.

James. 1994. "Letter." *EarthSpirit Community Newsletter,* July, 15.

Jenet. 1994a. "Becoming Men and Women." *The Labryinth* 2 (Imbolc): 2–3.

———. 1994b. "Track 1." *The Labryinth* 2 (Beltane): 4–5.

———. 1994c. "Track 5." *The Labryinth* 2 (Beltane): 11–13.

———. 1994d. "Track 3." *The Labryinth* 3 (Lammas): 8–9.

———. 1995a. "Track 3." *The Labryinth* 3 (Imbolc): 10–11.

———. 1995b. "Track 5." *The Labryinth* 3 (Imbolc): 14.

Jones, Richard A. 1996. "From the Beaumont Texas CUUPS Chapter." *Covenant of Unitarian Universalist Pagans Newsletter,* August.

Judith, Anodea. 1993. "Between the Worlds: Late Adolescence and Early Adulthood in Modern Paganism." In *Modern Rites of Passage: Witchcraft Today Book Two,* ed. Chas S. Clifton, 75–92. St. Paul, Minn.: Llewellyn Publications.

Keller, Evelyn Fox. 1985. *Reflections on Gender and Science.* New Haven: Yale University Press.

Kelly, Aidan A. 1991. *Crafting the Art of Magic: Book I.* St. Paul, Minn.: Llewellyn Publications.

———. 1992. "An Update on Neopagan Witchcraft in America." In *Perspectives on the New Age,* ed. James R. Lewis and J. Gordon Melton. Albany: State University of New York Press.

Kephart, William. 1982. *Extraordinary Groups: The Sociology of Unconventional Lifestyles.* 2d ed. New York: St. Martin's Press.

Kirkpatrick, George R., Rich Rainey, and Kathryn Rubi. 1986. "An Empirical Study of Wiccan Religion in Postindustrial Society." *Free Inquiry in Creative Sociology* 14 (1): 33–38.

Lakoff, Robin. 1976. *Language and Women's Place.* New York: Octagon Books.

Lasch, Christopher. 1991. *The Culture of Narcissim: American Life in an Age of Diminishing Expectations.* New York: Norton.

Lofland, John, and James Richardson. 1984. "Religious Movement Organizations: Elemental Forms and Dynamics." In *Research in Social Movements, Conflict and Change,* vol. 7, ed. K. Lang. Greenwich, Conn.: JAI Press, 29–51.

Luhrmann, T. M. 1989. *Persuasions of the Witch's Craft: Ritual Magic in Contemporary England.* Cambridge, Mass.: Harvard University Press.

Magical Rat. 1994. Internet communication on newsgroup Alt.Pagan, December 14.

Manor, Lisa Dugan. 1994. "Welcome to the Hundred Acre Wood." *Mezlim: Practical Magick for Today* 5 (4): 15–16.

Marty, Martin E. 1970. "The Occult Establishment." *Social Research* 37:212–30.

Marx, Karl. 1967. *Capital.* New York: International Publishers.

McArthur, Margie. 1994. *WiccaCraft for Families.* Langley, B.C.: Phoenix Publishing.

McGregor, Elisabeth. 1996. E-mail communication, December 8.

McGuire, Meredith B. 1988. *Ritual Healing in Suburban America.* New Brunswick, N.J.: Rutgers University Press.

———. 1992. *Religion: The Social Context.* 3d ed. Belmont, Calif.: Wadsworth.

———. 1994. "Gendered Spirituality and Quasi-Religious Ritual." In *Religion and the Social Order,* vol. 4, ed. Arthur L. Greil and Thomas Robbins. Greenwich Conn.: JAI Press.

Melton, J. Gordon. 1992. *Encyclopedic Handbook of Cults in America.* New York: Garland Publications.

Melucci, Alberto. 1985. "The Symbolic Challenge of Contemporary Movements." *Social Research* 52 (4): 789–816.

Merchant, Carolyn. 1980. *The Death of Nature: Women Ecology and the Scientific Revolution.* New York: Harper and Row.

Murray, Margaret A. [1921] 1971. *The Witch-Cult in Western Europe.* Reprint. Oxford: Clarendon Press.

————. 1977. *The God of the Witches*. London: Oxford University Press.

Neitz, Mary-Jo. 1991. "In Goddess We Trust." In *In Gods We Trust*, ed. Thomas Robbins and Dick Anthony, 353–72. New Brunswick, N.J.: Transaction Press.

————. 1994. "Quasi-religions and Cultural Movements: Contemporary Witchcraft as a Churchless Religion." In *Religion and The Social Order*, vol. 4, ed. Arthur L. Greil and Thomas Robbins. Greenwich, Conn.: JAI Press.

Niebuhr, Gustav. 1996. "Unitarians Striking Chord of Spirituality." *New York Times,* December 8, 28.

Niebuhr, H. Richard. 1929. *The Social Sources of Denominationalism.* New York: Henry Holt.

Northage-Orr, Althea. 1994. "Working with Children." *Mezlim: Practical Magick for Today* 5 (4): 6–9.

O'Gaea, Ashleen. 1993. *The Family Wicca Book*. St. Paul, Minn.: Llewellyn Publications.

Orion, Loretta. 1995. *Never Again the Burning Times: Paganism Revived*. Prospect Heights, Ill.: Waveland Press.

Palmer, Susan J. 1994. *Moon Sisters, Krishna Mothers, Rajneesh Lovers: Women's Roles in New Religions*. Syracuse, N.Y.: Syracuse University Press.

Phelan, Shane. 1995. *Getting Specific: Postmodern Lesbian Politics*. St. Paul, Minn.: University of Minnesota Press.

Pigman, Paul. 1991. "Dear Folks." *EarthSpirit Community Newsletter,* March, 15–18.

Pike, Sarah M. 1996. "Forging Magical Selves: Gendered Bodies and Ritual Fires at Neo-Pagan Festivals." In *Magical Religon and Modern Witchcraft*, ed. John R. Lewis. New York: State University of New York Press.

Pollitt, Katha. 1992. "Marooned on Gilligan's Island: Are Women Morally Superior to Men?" *The Nation,* December 28.

Rabinovitch, Shelley Tsivia. 1996. "Spells of Transformation: Categorizing Modern Neo-Pagan Witches." In *Magical Religion and Modern Witchcraft*, ed. James R. Lewis. Albany: State University of New York Press.

Ranck, Shirley Ann. 1995. *Cakes for the Queen of Heaven*. Chicago: Delphi Press.

————. 1996. Personal communication.

Rapaport, Lynn. 1997. *Jews in Germany after the Holocaust: Identity, Memory and Relations with Germans*. Cambridge, England: Cambridge University Press.

Raphael, Melissa. 1996. "Truth in Flux: Goddess Feminism as a Late Modern Religion." *Religion* 25:199–213.

Reuther, Rosemary Radford. 1983. *Sexism and God Talk*. Boston: Beacon Press.

Richardson, Alan. 1990. *Earth God Rising: The Return of the Male Mysteries*. St. Paul, Minn.: Llewellyn Publications.

Richardson, James T. 1979. "From Cult to Sect: Creative Eclecticism in New Religious Movements." *Pacific Sociological Review* 22 (2): 139–66.

————. 1985. "The Deformation of New Religions: Impacts of Societal and Organizational Factors." In *Cults, Culture and the Law*, ed. T. Robbins, W. Shepard, and J. McBride. Chico, Calif.: Scholars Press.

Robbins, Thomas. 1985. "New Religious Movements on the Frontier of Church and State." In *Cults, Culture and the Law,* ed. T. Robbins, W. Shepard, and J. McBride. Chico, Calif.: Scholars Press.

————. 1988. *Cults, Converts and Charisma.* London: Sage Publications.

Robbins, Thomas, and David Bromley. 1992. "Social Experimentation and the Significance of American New Religions: A Focused Review Essay." *Research in the Social Scientific Study of Religion* 4:1–28.

Robbins, Thomas, Dick Anthony, and James Richardson. 1978. "Theory and Research on Today's New Religions." *Sociological Analysis* 39 (2): 103–21.

Roberts, Richard H. 1995. "Globalised Religion?: The 'Parliament of the World's Religions' (Chicago 1993) in Theoretical Perspective." *Journal of Contemporary Religion* 10 (2): 121–38.

Rose, Elliot. 1962. *A Razor for a Goat.* Toronto: University of Toronto Press.

Rosenau, Pauline Marie. 1992. *Post-Modernism and the Social Sciences: Insights, Inroads and Intrusions.* Princeton: Princeton University Press.

Ross, Warren R. 1996. "Diversity without Division" *World: The Journal of the Unitarian Universalist Association* 10 (November/December): 32–37.

Rubin, Lillian B. 1985. *The Role of Friendship in Our Lives.* New York: Harper and Row.

————. 1990. *Erotic Wars: What Happened to the Sexual Revolution?* New York: Harper-Collins.

Russell, Jeffrey Burton. 1972. *Witchcraft in the Middle Ages.* Secaucus, N.J.: Citadel Press.

————. 1980. *A History of Witchcraft.* London: Thames and Hudson.

Serith, Ceisiwr. 1991. "Finding the Third Way: Becoming a Man." *EarthSpirit Community Newsletter,* Summer, 5–7.

————. 1994. *The Pagan Family: Handing the Old Ways Down.* St. Paul, Minn.: Llewellyn Publications.

Shutz, Alfred. 1964. *Collected Papers.* Vol. 2. The Hague: Martinus Nijhoff.

Simmel, George. 1906. "The Sociology of Secrecy and of Secret Societies." *The American Journal of Sociology* 11:441–98.

Sontag, Michael. 1994. "Children, Magick and Realism." *Mezlim: Practical Magick for Today* 5 (4): 12–13.

Stanford-Blake, Donna. 1994. "Pagan Parenting: My Perspective." *Mezlim: Practical Magick for Today* 5 (4): 21.

Starhawk. 1979. *The Spiral Dance.* New York: Harper and Row.

————. 1982. *Dreaming the Dark.* Boston: Beacon Press.

————. 1991. "Why Pagans May Be Conscientious Objectors to War." *EarthSpirit Community Newsletter,* March, 2–3.

Stark, Rodney, and William Bainbridge. 1985. *The Future of Religion.* Berkeley: University of California Press.

Stewart, Richard. 1996. "Some Unitarians Aren't Moonstruck with Pagans' Beliefs." *Houston Chronicle,* July 28.

Swilling, Paula. 1991. "To the EarthSpirit Community." *EarthSpirit Community Newsletter,* March, 12–14.

Teague, Holly. 1994. "Children: The Next Generation." *Mezlim: Practical Magick for Today* 5 (4): 19–20.

Tonnies, Ferdinand. 1957. *Community and Society.* New York: Harper and Row.

Trevor-Roper, H. R. 1969. *The European Witch Craze of the 16th and 17th Century and Other Essays.* New York: Harper and Row.

Truzzi, Marcello. 1972. "The Occult Revival as Popular Culture: Some Random Observations on the Old and the Nouveau Witch." *Sociological Quarterly* 13:17–24.

———. 1974. "Toward a Sociology of the Occult: Notes on Modern Witchcraft." In *Religious Movements in Contemporary America,* ed. Irving I. Zaretsky and Mark P. Leone. Princeton: Princeton University Press.

Turner, Victor. 1969. *The Ritual Process.* Chicago: Aldine.

Unitarian Universalist Association. 1996a. *Statement of Principles.* Boston: Unitarian Universalist Association.

———. 1996b. *1996–97 Directory.* Boston: Unitarian Universalist Association.

Wallis, Roy. 1977. *The Road to Total Freedom.* New York: Columbia University Press.

Warner, R. Stephen. 1993. "Work in Progress Toward a New Paradigm for the Sociological Study of Religion in the United States." *American Journal of Sociology* 98:1044–93.

———. 1994. "The Place of the Congregation in the Contemporary American Religious Configuration." In *American Congregations,* vol. 2, ed. James P. Wind and James W. Lewis. Chicago: University of Chicago Press.

Webber, M. 1970. "Order in Diversity: Community without Propinquity." In *Neighborhood, City and Metropolis,* ed. R. Gutman and D. Popenoe, 792–81. New York: Random House.

Weber, Max. 1964. *The Sociology of Religion.* Boston: Beacon Press.

Weiss, Penny A. 1995. "Feminist Reflections on Community." In *Feminism and Community,* ed. Penny A. Weiss and Marilyn Friedman. Philadelphia: Temple University Press.

White, Harlan. 1996. "Pagans Euphemized Under as Nature-Based Religion." *Covenant of Unitarian Universalist Pagans Newsletter,* August.

Willow. 1990. "An Open Letter to ESC." *EarthSpirit Community Newsletter,* October, 9–10.

Wrong, Dennis. 1976. *Skeptical Sociology.* London: Heinemann.

Yinger, J. M. 1970. *The Scientific Study of Religion.* New York: Macmillan.

INDEX

Abby, 87

Adler, Margot, 21, 61, 75, 76, 81, 101, 116, 119

affirmations, 60

Aidala, Angela, 45

Alan, Jim, 110

Alex, 90

Alexander, Scott, 117

Allen, Prudence, 45

all-women's groups, 13–14, 20, 37–38, 62, 123; gender roles in, 45; and hierarchy, 112

Anne, 96

Arachne, 11, 47, 48, 49, 51, 52, 55, 63–64, 121

Arthen, Andras Corban, 10–11, 15, 20, 34, 101; as administrator of the EarthSpirit Community, 104, 105–9, 111, 113; on *community,* 66

Arthen, Deirdre Pulgram, 89, 101; as administrator of the EarthSpirit Community, 104, 105–9

Arthen, Inanna, 103–4, 109, 113, 115–16, 117, 120, 121, 122, 130

Ashera, 26

Athanor Fellowship, 104

Bainbridge, William, 63, 104–5

Barker, Eileen, 5

Barry, 49–50

Beckford, James, 4, 5, 28–29, 101, 123, 124

Bellah, Robert, 70

Beltane, 17, 31, 44, 88; sexual aspects of, 93–94

Berger, Peter L., 4

Beth, 40, 48, 50, 63, 64

Beuhrans, Rev., 118

Bird, Fred, 108

Bonewits, Isaac, 24, 111, 113–14

Book of Shadows, 61

bookstores, as center for community, 77

Bowens-Wheatly, Marjorie, 117

Bromley, David, 37, 40, 127

Buckland, Raymond, 12

Cabot, Laurie, 32, 77

Cakes for the Queen of Heaven, 114

Candlemas, 18

Carol, 49, 64

Carpenter, Dennis, 110

Catholicism, 98

children: and magic and mysticism, 96–99; in the Neo-Pagan community, 14–15, 82–86; rites of passage for, 90–92; and rituals, 86–90; and sexuality, 92–96

Christianity, and Neo-Paganism, 16–17, 88, 98

Circle Network News, 110

Circle of Light coven, 11, 16–17, 24, 40, 44, 69, 121; establishment of, 47–49; life cycle of, 51–52; relationships within, 63–64; as training coven, 55–56

Circle Sanctuary, 110

client cults, 105

coercive isomorphism, 102, 103, 126

Cohen, Anthony P., 72

coincidence, 32

color, symbolism of, 2–3, 47
"coming out," 68, 98
community: building of, 72–77; definitions of, 65–66; in late modernity, 66–70, 80; lesbian, 68, 70; of memory, 70–71, 125; and mystical worldview, 69; notion of among Neo-Pagans, 65–66, 68–70, 124–25; and political activity, 77–81; as process, 67–68
Covenant of the Goddess (CoG), 94, 111
Covenant of the Unitarian Universalist Pagans (CUUPs), 100, 103, 129; development of, 114–16; impact on Unitarian Universalist Association, 119–20; similarities and differences with Unitarian Universalists, 116–19
covens: as congregation, 54–55; family as metaphor of, 50, 62–64; as friendship groups, 52–60, 124; hierarchy within, 62; intimacy within, 56–59, 64; membership in, 51; number of, 9; secrecy within, 61–62; size of, 9; standardization within, 103; training within, 51, 55–56, 60–61, 124. See also Circle of Light coven
crone, ritual for, 38
Cunningham, Scott, 101

Daniel, 50, 51
Danzger, M. Herbert, 98
Darling-Ferns, Zack, 95–96
death, celebration of, 17–18, 30–31, 89
Diana, ritual for, 37–38
DiMaggio, Paul, 102–3, 126
Dorothy (Old Dorothy), 11–12, 21
Doug, 79
Doyle, Ruth, 118
Drawing Down the Moon (Adler), 103
dreams, 29

Earth God Rising: The Return of the Male Mysteries (Richardson), 42
EarthSpirit Community, 29–30, 44–45, 59, 66; debate over funding for, 104–12
Easter, 88
eggs, symbolism of, 16–17
Egyptian religion, as part of Wiccan ancestry, 20, 21
Eilberg-Schwartz, Howard, 5–6
Eller, Cynthia, 38
Eluba, 98, 99
Enlightenment tradition: and goddess movement, 5–6; and Wicca, 6, 123, 130
esabats, 18
essentialism, 45

The Family Wicca Book (O'Gaea), 85
Farrar, Janet, 41–42
Farrar, Stewart, 41–42
feminist movement, and sexuality, 92
feminist spirituality, and Neo-Paganism, 13, 114
festivals, 72–77; attendance at, 75–76; rituals at, 74–75. See also Rites of Spring
Finley, Nancy J., 13–14
FireHeart, 104, 109, 112
Fox, Selena, 101, 110
Freud, Sigmund, 29
friendships within the coven, 52–60, 124
Frost, Gavin, 94
Frost, Robert, 54
Frost, Yvonne, 94

Gabriel, 24, 33, 47, 48, 51, 55, 60, 63–64, 121
Gail, 49
Galbreath, Robert, 19–20
Gardner, Gerald, 11–12, 13, 14, 16, 43
gender roles in Wicca: in all-women's groups, 45; and homosexuality,

43–45; men's, 40–43; polarity of,
43–44; views of, 45–46; women's,
37–40
Gergen, Kenneth J., 124
Giddens, Anthony, 6–8, 28, 35, 36,
53, 78, 79, 80, 102, 124
Glainn Sidhr Order of Witches, 104,
105
god, within Wiccan mythology, 42–43
goddess: as image in Wicca, 32–33,
41; worship of, 41, 46
goddess movement, 5–6, 13, 22–23,
24, 114
Gordon, 87
Greil, Arthur L., 5, 55
Griffin, Wendy, 37–38

Habits of the Heart (Bellah et al.), 70
handfastings, 33
Harrow, Judy, 66, 111, 112, 113
Hawkins, Jaq, 85, 89
Hermetic Order of the Golden Dawn,
21
Hicks, Brad, 22
Hildebrand, Jerrie, 115, 116
Hillery, George, 65
Holocaust, 22, 70–71
homosexuality, 43–45
How About Magic (HAM), 87, 91

Icarus, 26
Imbolc, 18, 89–90
individual, as agent, 7–8. *See also* self-
identity; self-transformation
information, sharing of, 77, 100, 122,
125
initiation ritual, 1–3, 87
Internet, Wiccan sites on, 76
isomorphism, types of: as mechanisms
for homogenization, 102–3;
applied to Wicca, 103–4, 111, 112,
126

Jenet, 85, 86, 87, 91, 93, 98

Jerry, 33
Joan, 97
Joe, 22, 45
John, 24
Judith, 96
Judy, 29, 79

Keller, Evelyn Fox, 23–24
Kelly, Aidan, 9
Kirkpatrick, George R., 9

The Labyrinth, 85
Laima, 26–27
Lakoff, Robin, 57
Lammas, 17
Larry, 46
lesbians: in all-women's groups, 14; as
community, 68–69, 70, 77
Levy, Ruth, 70
Linda, 22, 49, 51, 56, 60, 62–63, 76,
103
Lisa, 87
Luhrmann, T. M., 12, 20, 31, 33–34

magic: as aspect of Witchcraft, 15,
18–21; as experienced at festivals,
74–75; and Neo-Pagan children,
96–99; psychological component
of, 34; and routinization, 101; and
science, 23–24
Marty, Martin E., 15
Mary, ritual for, 38
Mayfire, Bonnie, 83
Mayfire, David, 40–41, 42
Mayfire, Shara, 83
Mayfire family: affiliation with
Unitarian Universalists, 83, 115;
maypole rituals, 44; symbolism of, 17
McGregor, Elisabeth, 119
McGuire, Meredith B., 4, 5, 36, 61–
62
Melanie, 32
men, gender roles in Wicca, 40–43
methodology of study, xi–xvi

Meyer, Suzanne, 116, 117
mimetic isomorphism, 102, 103, 111, 126
modernity, late: community in, 66–70; self-identity in, 28–29; Wicca as religion of, 6–8, 102, 123–24, 125
moon cycles, 18
MoonTide Coven, 26–27, 97; saining ritual, 90–91
MotherChant, 107–8
Murray, Margaret, 12, 21
mystery schools, 20
mysticism, and self-transformation, 31–34

naming ritual, 26–27, 29, 35–36
nature, reverence for, 16–17
Neitz, Mary-Jo, 13, 14, 52, 61–62
Neo-Paganism, 9–11, 12–13; and all-women's groups, 13–14; children in, 14–15, 82–86; church envisioned for, 120–21; festivals, 66, 72–77; notion of community among adherents, 65–66, 68–70, 124–25; and Rites of Spring, 59–60, 66; survey of adherents, 8–9, 14–15; and the Unitarian Universalist Association, 114–20, 126. See also Wicca; Witches
New Age religions, 5
newborn, initation of, 1–3
Nieburh, H. Richard, 122
normative isomorphism, 102, 103, 112, 126
Northage-Orr, Althea, 88
nudity, 94

occult knowledge, 19–20
O'Gaea, Ashleen, 85–86, 96–97, 98
omens, 20
organizational theory, and model for routinization of Wicca, xii, 102–4
Oriethyia, 111, 112, 113
Orion, Loretta, 5, 12, 20–21, 37, 123

Oscar, 49, 51, 56–57, 58, 60
Ostava, 16–17

"The Pagan Census," 8–10, 14–15, 36, 43, 50, 75, 83
Palmer, Susan J., 45
Parliament of World Religions, 130
Phelan, Shane, 67–68
Phillips, Lesley, 114, 129
physics, and Witchcraft, 23–24
Pike, Sarah M., 46
Pinti, Linda, 114, 129
politics: emancipatory politics, 78; life politics, 78–80, 125, 130; Witches' involvement in, 78–80, 125
postmodern theory: and religion, 5–6; and Wicca, 6–8
Powell, Walter, 102–3, 126
professionalization, 102; within Wicca, 103–4, 126
puberty, rituals surrounding, 90–92

Rapaport, Lynn, 70–71
Raphael, Melissa, 5–6, 80, 125
Real Magic (Bonewits), 24
Reclaiming Collective, 111
Rede, Wiccan, 8, 113
religion: definitions of, 4–5; and historical roots of Wicca, 20–23; postmodern theory and, 5–6; prophet's role in, 101; routinization of, 100–101; Wicca as, 4–6, 15, 52, 80–81, 83–84, 123–24
Renenutet, 26, 38
Richardson, Alan, 42
Richardson, James T., 108
Rise Up and Call Her Name, 114
rites of passage, 18, 90–92
Rites of Spring, 59–60, 73, 82–83, 106, 109–10
rituals, 16–18; Beltane, 17, 31, 44, 88, 93–94; children as part of, 86–90; and Christian holidays, 88;

celebrating death, 17–18, 30–31, 89; as creative acts, 100; croning, 38; fertility, 82–83; at festivals, 74–75; fires, 74–75; involving gender, 36, 37–40, 43–45; Imbolc, 18, 89–90; initiation, 1–3, 87; Lammas, 17; naming, 26–27, 29, 35–36; Ostava, 16–17; saining, 90–91; Samhain, 17–18, 29–31, 89; and self-transformation, 29–31, 35–36, 46; vernal equinox, 16, 47–48; wiccaning, 1–3, 90; Yule, 18

Robbins, Thomas, 5, 37, 40, 127

Ron, 22

routinization: of religion, 100–101; of Wicca, 100, 101–4, 121–22, 126–27

Rubin, Lillian B., 53, 54, 93

Rudy, David R., 55

sabbats, 29–30. *See also* rituals

saining, 90–91

Samhain, 17–18, 29–31, 89

Satan, 11

science, magic and, 23–24

seasons, rituals associated with, 16–18

self-identity: as framed in context of Wicca, 5, 7–8, 10–11, 124; and friendships, 53–54; and gender, 36–46; in modernity, 28–29; rituals of, 29–31

self-transformation, 27–28, 124; within communities of choice, 67; healing as part of, 38; and mystical worldview, 31–34; rituals of, 29–31, 35–36. *See also* gender roles in Wicca

Serith, Ceisiwr, 43, 86, 87–88, 91

sexuality: celebration of, 17; and children, 92–96. *See also* gender roles; homosexuality

sexual revolution, 92–93

Shutz, Alfred, 69

Simmel, George, 62

skepticism, 24

solo practitioners, 50–51

Sontag, Michael, 84

The Spiral Dance (Starhawk), 103

spring equinox, 16–17, 47. *See also* Ostava

Starhawk, 23, 54, 57, 60, 61, 71, 76, 111

Stark, Rodney, 63, 104–5

Steve, 49, 55, 64

structuration theory: as framework for understanding Wicca, 6–8, 102

Susan, 97

Tammy, 50–51

Teague, Holly, 84–85

Three Blade Jaguar, 26–27, 35–36

Truzzi, Marcello, 15

Unitarian Universalist Association: and Baptist churches, 117–18; and Neo-Paganism, 103, 114–20, 129. *See also* Covenant of the Unitarian Universalist Pagans

Unitarian Universalist Church, 83

Valiente, 12

Walking with Mother Earth (Arthen), 89

Wallis, Roy, 108

Warner, R. Stephen, 122

Weber, Max, 100–101

Webster, Sam, 111–12, 113

weddings, 33

Westley, Frances, 108

White Water. *See* Three Blade Jaguar

Wicca: and all-women's groups, 13–14, 37–38, 123; charismatic leaders in, 101; children as part of, 14–15, 82–86, 126, 128; congregational structure for, 120–21, 130; demographics of adherents, 8–10, 14–15, 36–37; derivation of word, 11;

Wicca (*continued*)
and environmentalism, 8, 16, 22, 72, 78–79, 81, 123, 124; female participants in, 36–40; and feminism, 8, 46, 57, 72, 123, 124; finances as issue in, 104–12, 121, 128–29; future of, 127–30; Gerald Gardner's influence on, 11–12, 14, 16; goddess as image in, 32–33, 41; hierarchies within, 112–13, 121–22; and inclusive groups, 14, 45, 123; magic as aspect of, 15, 18–21; male participants in, 37, 40–43; mythical roots of, 20–23, 71–72, 125; neophytes in, 61; and notion of community, 65–66, 68–70, 124–25; and politics, 78–80, 125; professionalization within, 103–4, 126; as religion, 4–6, 15, 52, 80–81, 83–84, 123–24; rituals as important to, 16–18; routinization of, 100, 101–4, 121–22, 126–27; sexuality within, 92–96; standardization within, 103; training in, 51, 55–56, 60–61, 113; in the United States, 9–10, 12–15. *See also* covens; EarthSpirit Community; Neo-Paganism; rituals; Witches

wiccaning, 1–3, 90
Wiccan Rede, 8, 113
Willow, 107
Witch: defined, 11; negative stereotypes associated with, 85, 99
Witchcraft. *See* Wicca
Witches: as community, 69–70; political activity of, 77–81; as solo practitioners, 50–51; training for, 51, 55–56, 60–61, 113; trials of, 71–72; worldview of, 23–25. *See also* covens; Wicca
Witches and Witchlings, 87
Witches' Anti-Defamation League, 77, 78
The Witch's Bible (Frost and Frost), 94
Witch's Rune, 61
women: gender roles in Wicca, 37–40
women's spirituality groups, 22–23

Yinger, J. M., 4
Yule, 18, 88; songs for, 103

Zack, 91–92